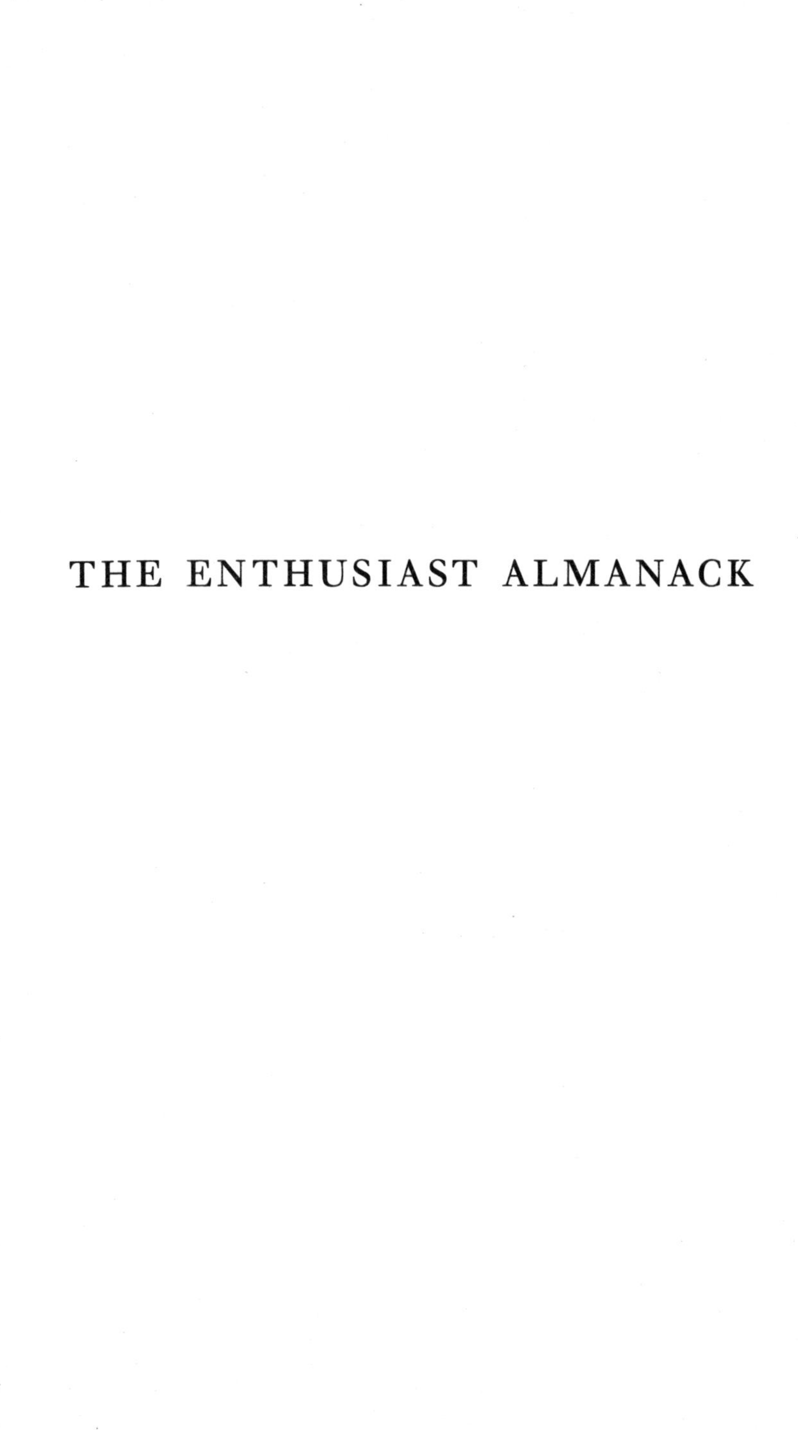

THE ENTHUSIAST ALMANACK

THE ENTHUSIAST ALMANACK

Plain Living and *High Thinking*

Quercus

First published in Great Britain in 2006 by
Quercus
46 Dorset Street
London
WIU 7NB

DESIGN: VALLE WALKLEY

A CIP catalogue reference for this book is available from the British Library
ISBN 1-905204-49-3

10 9 8 7 6 5 4 3 2 1

- TABLE OF CONTENTS -

Welcome

You're going to like it. You don't know it yet, but you're going to like it.

It's Spring 2006 and here in the hut the mood is calm, and confident; the fan heater's cranking up. The visitors have arrived and almost to a person they know what they need is not what they want and, really, they're no trouble. The whole thing is kicking off somewhere towards the near horizon; the grass has started to grow back, which is a bonus and a blessing; and over at the supermarket two men have started a fight, punching and kicking seven shades and the living daylights out of each other, in the name, as the prophet said, of vengeance. A supermarket trolley slips aimlessly into a busy main road. And everywhere that anybody looks the signs are that winter has not been for nothing: the berries, for instance, who in their right mind would have thought of those? And the leaves, the leaves are a nice touch, though to be honest they might have shown up a little earlier. And there's a dog, barking–who knows, maybe a point of reference? Woof, he barks. Woof. Woof. WOOF.

And here–there, look, right there–you can feel it, that's the inclination starting up again, the stirring, that sensation that if you ever allowed it to might threaten to become a surge, which it's always good to damp down because what it seems to promise is pleasure, optimism even, which let's face it you either plump for or you don't, and mostly you don't: bafflement, maybe, at best you go for; or maybe ruin postponed. But away over in the park the ducks don't care: lowering, lowering, lowering, landing, running along the surface of the water for a moment before surfing freely to a halt. Like mad things. Like they just discovered they were in their element. Saturday, 25th March. As good a day for it, perhaps, as any.

And so, and anyway, like all magazines *The Enthusiast* emerged to meet a gap in the market. Many subjects were already well catered for: photography, books, sex, gossip, emerging markets, software, sex, politics, hotel management, sex, gaming, international relations, blood sports, quad bikes, sex, God. Skilfully, they all managed to be remarkably similar, while seeming just a little bit different. They carried glossy photographs, and interviews with minor celebrities, with people who were on television, or who liked to think of themselves as being on television. They had barcodes and they sat on shelves, and people read them on trains, and then they turned up in waiting rooms. And so the demand was met.

Joy, though, well: that's another matter entirely; another market segment; another niche. There's the joy of sex, of course, but frankly if you were to go up to the woman at the counter and you were to say, 'Do you know what I'm really looking for? What I'm looking for is not this,' and you were to toss down that magazine and you were to say, 'What I'm looking for is something joyous, a really optimistic kind of a magazine,' you know what you'd get? A blank look. If you were lucky. Because no such magazine exists–or existed. 'And when I say optimism,' you might further try to explain, 'I don't mean anything easily won, I mean, you know, that gnarled kind of optimism, that optimism which knows that failure is always possible, but that nothing was ever achieved without venturing ruin, and that variousness is the last refuge of the human spirit, and that pessimism is the work of elites who want to keep the riches of human existence to themselves–a raging, roving, unpredictable optimism. That's what I want.' 'Next, please.' It was clear: a gap in the market had emerged.

And so *The Enthusiast* was born, not so much an answer as a question, something that knew the value of a good meal; and the work of many hands; and the product of years of speculation; and improvisation based on experience; and some solutions to some long, long-neglected problems; and a quarterly event; through whose many constituent parts ran a dense and, we all hoped, a humane philosophy, an inquiry into the prospects for mankind. And some people thought we were joking; and some people know that we're not. Either way it's here, it's yours: *The Enthusiast Almanack*, or *Omnibus*, or what you will. And you may make of it what you will. And you will. You will. You will. You will.

– CORRECTIONS AND CLARIFICATIONS –

SORRY, again, you were right and we were wrong : the children of the rich *do* deserve better ; because money *is* a merit ; and no of course we're not masters of our destiny ; and alright, yes, if you insist, maybe perfection is possible, with practice, surgery, or an endowment from a grant-making trust ; and probably all that separates us *is* a punch on the nose ; and no, of course, the permanent deep dark underground is not good for our complexion ; and yes, it's all very well treading the very gates of hell, but what is the point of working out your own salvation if there's no effective marketing or distribution ; and alas if it's gloss and not emulsion then no, it won't come out in the wash.

Any errors?

theenthusiast@theenthusiast.co.uk THE ENTHUSIAST, PO BOX 239, BANGOR, BT20 5YB

ANNOUNCEMENTS AND ADVERTISEMENTS—

The Enthusiast is Britain's fastest-growing magazine and is seeking part-time distributors and a business manager (see page 67) to work alongside its current staff.

If you believe you've got what it takes, contact *The Enthusiast*, PO Box 239, Bangor, BT20 5YB, theenthusiast@theenthusiast.co.uk

– ADVICE –

The force of a true knock-out depends not so much upon the strength of the arms but upon the swing of the body from the hips.

KELVIN GORDON *(Knaresborough)*

Fit the hole to the plant, not the plant to the hole.

MRS. MACLAREN *(Cockfosters)*

Any breach of a rule is a foul.

S.C. BLACKWELL *(Carlisle)*

In the south, shallots will be ripening where planted early in February. The soil should be pulled away from the cloves a little to assist ripening. Then hoe gently between the rows of garlic as these will soon be ready for harvesting.

HARRY SHERMAN *(Prenton)*

Particularly at this time of year, chronic drunkenness should neither be encouraged nor tolerated. Large doses of alcoholic liquors act like narcotic poisons and can cause death. I am myself a recovering alcoholic and would like to warn people through your magazine of the dangers of the 'demon' drink.

MR. B. BURKE *(Eaglesham)*

In an emergency a cricket bat may be used as a splint. I can testify to this personally.

G.F. DUNLOP *(Drogheda)*

After the age of thirty vigorous exercise should not be undertaken until after consultation with a doctor.

DR. M. MCMICHAEL *(Chepstow)*

No need for a fancy barber's shop. All you need are sharp kitchen scissors, a steady hand, and a tea-towel round the neck. My family have always cut each other's hair. We must have saved thousands of pounds.

E. GREEN *(Keynsham)*

Where water is necessary it should be done with care. Remember that once a plant is artificially watered it becomes dependent on such supplies. Do not water until you must, and then give a good soaking.

VERA WOOD *(Chelsea)*

Plan Ahead. Prepare your ground now to double next year's production.

GORDON GRIMLEY *(Hartlepool)*

Johnny Wisdom?

theenthusiast@theenthusiast.co.uk

THE ENTHUSIAST, PO BOX 239, BANGOR, BT20 5YB

- TRAVEL -

A POSTCARD FROM JAPAN

So here I am, sitting in Tokyo,
drinking cappuccino, and listening
to Bob Marley, checking my mail.
You know, there's juice in the old girl yet.

MARGARET CUNNINGHAM *(Kingsbridge)*

The Enthusiast invites postcards from around the world

THE ENTHUSIAST
PO BOX 239
BANGOR
BT20 5YB
theenthusiast@theenthusiast.co.uk

LETTERS

Sir — You're all too fat.
Yours faithfully, MR. T. CULLEN *(Dublin)*

Something to add?

theenthusiast@theenthusiast.co.uk THE ENTHUSIAST, PO BOX 239, BANGOR, BT20 5YB

- THE ESSENTIAL PHRASE BOOK -

Are you in earnest?

Parlez-vous sérieusement?

Sprechen sie im Ernst?

Lo dite sal serio?

EMILY LEADBETTER *(Ascot)*

Well?

theenthusiast@theenthusiast.co.uk THE ENTHUSIAST, PO BOX 239, BANGOR, BT20 5YB

- HEALTH -

WHY I QUIT THE GYM: A TRUE STORY

I USED TO WANT TO BE THIN. I weigh in now at a steady 227 pounds, wear outsize trousers, and shirts that over-hang. I'm not proud, but I am comfortable. Teleologically speaking I would say I have arrived at my end. Until recently, though, I wanted to be thin. I wanted to be thinner than thin ; I wanted to be among the thinnest. I wanted to move with the thin and know their secrets. The world divides. My place was with the thin.

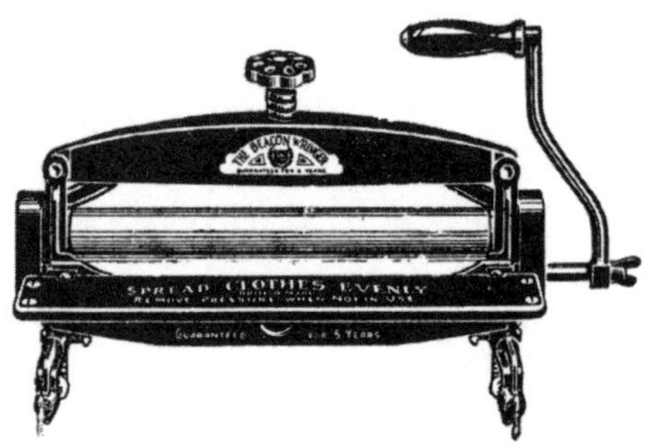

Threefold manifestation: "His Word" chap. 1. 3; "His Grace" chap. 2. 11; "His Glory" chap. 2. 13

St. Pauls theme - Faith. St. Peters theme - Hope. St. Johns theme - Love.

The Threefold Gift: He gave Himself for the Church Ep 5. 25. He gave Himself for us chap. 2. 14. He gave Himself for me. Gal 2. 20.

The Epistle of PAUL the Apostle to TITUS.

"Sobriety" 5 times

A. D. 65.

CHAPTER I.

PAUL, a servant of God, and an apostle of Jesus Christ, according to the faith of God's elect, and the acknowledging[a] of the truth which[b] is after godliness;

2 [β]In hope of eternal life, which God, that[c] cannot lie, promised before[d] the world began;

3 But[e] hath in due times manifested his word through preaching,[f] which is committed unto me, according to the commandment of God our Saviour;

4 To Titus, mine own son after the common faith: Grace, mercy, and peace, from God the Father and the Lord Jesus Christ our Saviour.

5 For this cause left I thee in Crete, that thou shouldest set in order[p] the things that are [ζ]wanting, and ordain[r] elders in every city, as I had appointed thee:

6 If any be blameless, the husband of one wife, having faithful children, not accused of riot, or unruly.

7 For a bishop[s] must be blameless, as the steward of God; not selfwilled, not soon angry, not given to wine, no striker, not given to filthy lucre;

8 But a lover of hospitality, a lover of good [η]men, sober, just, holy, temperate;

9 Holding[a] fast the faithful word, [θ]as he hath been taught, that he may be able by sound doctrine both to exhort and to convince the gainsayers.

10 For there are many unruly and vain talkers[d] and deceivers, specially they of the circumcision:

11 Whose mouths must be stopped; who subvert[e] whole houses, teaching things which they ought not, for filthy lucre's sake.

12 One[f] of themselves, even a prophet of their own, said, The Cretians are alway liars, evil beasts, slow bellies.

13 This witness is true. Wherefore rebuke[h] them sharply; that they may be sound in the faith;

14 Not giving heed to Jewish fables,[i] and commandments of men, that turn from the truth.

15 Unto[l] the pure all things are pure: but unto them that are defiled and unbelieving is nothing pure; but even their mind and conscience is defiled.

16 They profess[n] that they know God; but in works they deny him, being abominable, and disobedient, and unto every good work [μ]reprobate.

CHAPTER II.

BUT speak thou the things which become sound doctrine:

2 That the aged[q] men be [ν]sober, grave, temperate, sound in faith, in charity, in patience.

3 The aged women likewise, that they be in behaviour as becometh [ξ]holiness, not [π]false accusers, not given to much wine, teachers of good things;

4 That they may teach the young women to be [ρ]sober, to love their husbands, to love their children,

5 To be discreet, chaste, keepers at home, good, obedient to their own husbands, that the word of God be not blasphemed.

6 Young men likewise exhort to be [τ]sober minded:

7 In all things shewing thyself[t] a pattern of good works: in doctrine shewing uncorruptness, gravity, sincerity,

8 Sound[u] speech, that cannot be condemned; that he that is of the contrary part may be ashamed, having no evil thing to say of you.

9 Exhort servants[b] to be obedient unto their own masters, and to please them well in all things; not [γ]answering again;

10 Not purloining, but shewing all good fidelity; that[c] they may adorn the doctrine of God our Saviour in all things.

11 For the grace[d] of God that bringeth salvation [δ]hath appeared to all men,

12 Teaching us, that, denying[k] ungodliness and worldly lusts,[m] we[n] should live soberly, righteously, and godly, in this present world;

13 Looking[o] for that blessed hope, and the glorious appearing[q] of the great God and our Saviour Jesus Christ;

14 Who gave[r] himself for us, that he might redeem us from all[s] iniquity, and purify[u] unto himself a peculiar[v] people, zealous[w] of good works.

15 These things speak, and exhort, and rebuke with all authority. Let[y] no man despise thee.

CHAPTER III.

PUT them in mind to be subject[a] to principalities and powers, to obey magistrates, to be ready to every good work,

2 To speak evil of no man, to be no brawlers, but gentle, shewing all[b] meekness unto all men.

3 For[c] we ourselves also were sometimes foolish, disobedient, deceived, serving divers lusts and pleasures, living in malice and envy, hateful, and hating one another.

4 But after that the kindness and [κ]love of God our Saviour toward man appeared,

5 Not[f] by works of righteousness which we have done, but according to his mercy he saved us, by the washing of regeneration, and renewing of the Holy Ghost;

6 Which he shed on us [λ]abundantly, through Jesus Christ our Saviour;

7 That, being justified[k] by his grace, we should be made heirs according to the hope of eternal life.

8 This is a faithful saying, and these things I will that thou affirm constantly, that they which have believed in God might be careful[m] to maintain good works. These things are good and profitable unto men.

9 But[o] avoid foolish questions, and genealogies, and contentions, and strivings about the law; for they are unprofitable and vain.

10 A man that is an heretic, after the first and second admonition[p] reject;

11 Knowing that he that is such is subverted, and sinneth, being condemned of himself.

12 When I shall send Artemas unto thee, or Tychicus, be diligent to come unto me to Nicopolis: for I have determined there to winter.

13 Bring Zenas the lawyer and Apollos on their journey diligently, that nothing be wanting unto them.

14 And let our's also learn to [σ]maintain good[s] works for necessary uses, that they be not unfruitful.

15 All that are with me salute thee. Greet them that love us in the faith. Grace be with you all. Amen.

It was written to Titus, ordained the first bishop of the church of the Cretians, from Nicopolis of Macedonia.

---

a 2 Ti. 2. 25. b Ep. 6. 5, &c. c 1 Ti. 6. 3. β or, For. γ or, gainsaying. d 1 Sa. 15. 29. He. 6. 18. e Mat. 25. 34. f Mat. 5. 16. g 2 Ti. 1. 10. h Ro. 10. 14, 15 i Ro. 5. 15. δ or, to all men, hath appeared. k Ro. 8. 13. l 1 Ti. 1. 1, 2. m 1 Pe. 2. 11. n Lu. 1. 75. o 2 Pe. 3. 12. p 1 Co. 11. 34. q Re. 1. 7. ζ or, left undone. r Ac. 14. 23. 2 Ti. 2. 2. s Ep. 5. 2. t Ps. 130. 8. u He. 9. 14. v De. 7. 6. 1 Pe. 2. 9. w Ep. 2. 10. x 1 Ti. 3. 2, &c. y 1 Ti. 4. 12. z Ro. 13. 1. η or, things. a 2 Th. 2. 15. θ or, in teaching. b Ep. 4. 2. c 1 Co. 6. 11. 1 Pe. 4. 3. d Ja. 1. 26. e Mat. 23. 14. κ or, pity. f Ac. 17. 28. g Ep. 2. 4, 8, 9. h 2 Ti. 4. 2. λ or, richly. i 1 Ti. 1. 4. k Ro. 3. 24. l Ro. 14. 14, 20 m ver. 1, 14. n 2 Ti. 3. 5, 7. o 2 Ti. 2. 23. μ or, void of judgment. p Mat. 18. 17. q Pr. 16. 31. ν or, vigilant. ξ or, holy women. π or, makebates. r 1 Ti. 5. 14. ρ or, wise. σ or, profess honest trades. s verse 8. τ or, discreet. t 1 Ti. 4. 12. u 1 Ti. 6. 3.

Workless Faith God never regards. Faithless Work God never rewards.

Holdfast Sound Words 1 Tim 1. 13. Strive not about Words 1 Tim 2. 14. Rightly dividing the Word 1 Tim 2. 15.

Ready in every Good Work ch 3. 1. Fruitful in every Good Work Col 1. 21. Perfect in every Good Work Heb 13. 2.

Not that I was naïve. Thin is a conspiracy. In an age without religion, thin is guilt. Fat is gluttony, naturally, and so it follows that thin—guilt-driven bodily self-denial—comes complete with the promise of salvation. Not eternal salvation, of course, not a never-ending life to follow a life of ultimate dedication, but a few extra years where otherwise there would be a diseased heart, an extra decade maybe, in the company of strangers. And not that they would be happy years ; quite likely they would be lean, the mind slipping into itself and the body giving way, slumped forward in an uncomfortable arm-chair, smelling slightly, dribbling a little. Still, though, the equations are clear : fat, early death ; thin, long life. And since long life is always the reward, then fat is a stigma, and so like everybody who was anybody I went to the gym.

Maybe one day, if they haven't already, the people who plan these things will cotton on ; that actually—all Judaeo-Christian mythology notwithstanding—it isn't such a great idea for everybody to be so healthy in middle life. There are, after all, only so many dribbling old ladies the state can afford, even at the present rudimentary levels of care. It's hard to think of a unit more greedy of resources than an old lady dribbling, more hopelessly and fundamentally unproductive. And so at some point, if it hasn't already, the thought might occur that where the message was always thin it ought to be fat. Think not what your country can do for you, eat rich, die young. This, however, would be to overlook the gym.

The gym is pivotal. In my own case there would be phases, maybe six weeks at a time say, when I would manage something like a regular and acceptable level of attendance ; only then I would lapse, and another six weeks would go by and the sugars and carbohydrates would begin to accrete around my waist, which I could largely conceal, and around my jowls, which I couldn't ; and so driven by guilt I would return for what could only be called penance, running and rowing until I thought my heart would surely burst ; offering up toxins in return for forgiveness ; making my peace with a monitoring God. Except that if its logic is religious, the truth of the gym, as I attended just regularly enough to know, was elsewhere. The truth of the gym—as I began to appreciate, as I drove myself forwards, as I fought my inertia—is work. The truth of everything is work—I work, you work, he works, she works, they watch us work. The more I began to think about it, however, the more it dawned on me that of all modern social phenomena, the gym tells us the truth about work.

The trouble, I realised, is that the working day is too short. This hasn't always been the case. In the middle of the nineteenth century, for instance, the working day was a convenient length, twelve hours on average, leaving just enough time for a person to get home, eat and sleep. Convenient because, well, you knew where people were when they were at work, who they were mixing with and what they were stirring up. Except that people being people they wouldn't wear it ; and anyway when on earth were they to spend the money they earned on the goods they had made if seven till seven they were producing. The model citizen, after all, is both consumer and producer, and so the working day was shortened and people were called upon to shop.

The call was loud and nobody could avoid it. For some it was a form of inspiration. Other people—women mostly—were set aside whose function it was exclusively to shop. Actually, though, as it turned out, there is only so much shopping a person can do. This varied, obviously, according to temperament and income, but on average, after the work and the shopping had been done, there was time left for rumination. And there again not everybody ruminated, although it was surprise to all concerned just how many did. The high point of rumination was the 1960s. It was in the 1960s that the planners introduced the gym.

And so at a stroke a new category was born—I tried to explain this once to the person on the next-door bike, but as I got to the word 'stroke' I became audibly breathless ; he looked alarmed for a moment, and then he pedalled on. Leisure-work. It *is* leisure because nobody actually compels you to attend, although associates tell me there are blue-chip workplaces which have their own gym, a company benefit, like private health insurance—which you would need, clearly, in the last, dribbling decade of your life. But it is also work. And not even 'also'—the qualification somehow misses the point. The gym—and this is the genius and the tragedy of the place—is work in its purest, least corrupted form.

**'I TRY ALL THINGS;
I ACHIEVE WHAT I CAN.'**

HERMAN MELVILLE—(Moby-Dick)

Previously for pure work—if you really wanted to work a person hard, if your single-minded object was to get something out of them—probably you couldn't do better than the factory. There were drawbacks of course—the gradual build-up of human resistance, the common cause generated by the common place—but on the whole, what with its divisions of labour, the manifest dominance of the machinery,

and the always apparent sense of physical and psychological threat, the factory was good if what you were looking for was to concentrate the mind on the task at hand. These days, with the decline and then recent passing of heavy labour, there are few places left where a person can subdue themselves in the face of a machine. Not that anybody would have predicted that this would be a matter of regret. Except clearly it is—collectively, unconsciously—and so night after night, at the end of the working day, people subject themselves to the lost reality of manufacturing : the clank of metal against metal, the iron discipline of the clock.

It took me a while—probably I was down to 160 by this point, elasticated T-shirts clinging promisingly to my chest—but when finally it came to me, that the gym is nostalgia for the factory, it was with the awful certainty of a new artistic truth. What I couldn't see was why. I was at loss for a motive. Why, I would ask myself, as I pounded Xeno-like towards the mirror, should a society only recently liberated from the worst excesses of industry, set out nightly to live the whole abject experience over again. Revenge was a possibility. Maybe, after two hundred years of domination, people were resolved now the tables had finally been turned, to get their own back, establish who really was boss here, finally to triumph over the dead-weight of the machine. Maybe, by this way of thinking, all that voluntary pulling and pumping was the residue of a struggle that hadn't been satisfactorily won. One day, after all, people were sat there hating the lump of iron into which they were pouring every useful minute of their life ; the next it was gone, and they wanted closure. Except that as I looked around me what I saw weren't vengeful people. Driven, to be sure, but not by a historical sense of grudge. And so the explanation was what? That people tethered themselves to technology because they liked it, got a kick out of acquiescing to the products of their own brains. And which meant the Industrial Revolution was what? The fulfilment of a collective human fantasy? I stepped sweating but alive from the still circulating treadmill. 'This is a factory,' I shouted. 'And you are its products ; target hungry citizens of a post-industrial world. You were born figments of the brain of Martin Luther. Eat rich I tell you ; die young.' I walked out, euphoric, and promptly handed in my membership. The woman at the desk was reading Thomas Mann.

'*Death in Venice*?'

She nodded, coyly.

The thought occurred to me she could use a few pounds.

NORMAN PIPER *(Axminster)*

Exercised?

theenthusiast@theenthusiast.co.uk

THE ENTHUSIAST, PO BOX 239, BANGOR, BT20 5YB

LIVES OF THE FAMOUS

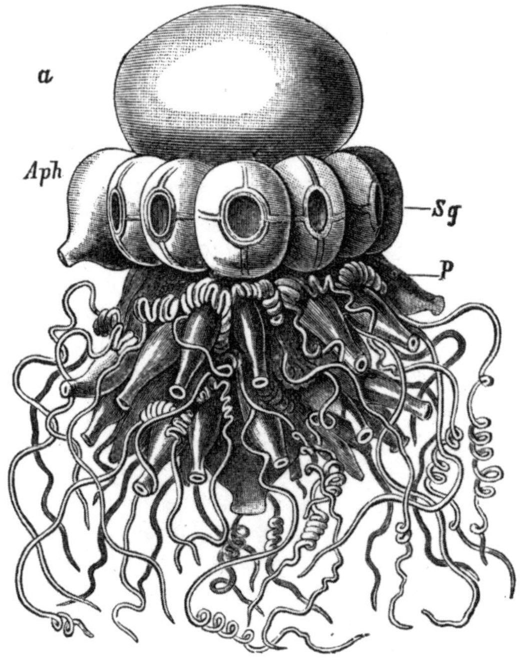

THOMAS MORE—The strangest exhibit on show at the quincentennial exhibition for Sir Thomas More at the National Portrait Gallery was undoubtedly a reliquary containing a fragment of his hair shirt. No one knows when More first began to wear a hair shirt but Thomas Stapleton speaks of him doing so 'even in youth'. In a letter of 1535 John Bouge tells of how More's wife Dame Alice had asked him to beg More to stop wearing the shirt, since it 'tamyd hys fleshe tyll the blod was sene in hys clothes'. In Roper's *Life of More* we discover that for the avoiding of singularity More did not wish his habit to be known. However, Roper records how one summer Anne Cresacre was sitting with More, who was dressed 'singly in his doublert and hose'. Cresacre spotted the hair shirt and began to laugh. Roper goes on, 'My wife, not ignorant of his manner, perceyuinge the same, pryvily told him of it; and he, beinge sory that she sawe it, presently amended it.'

JOHN SCOTT *(Bromley)*

Tamed flesh?

theenthusiast@theenthusiast.co.uk THE ENTHUSIAST, PO BOX 239, BANGOR, BT20 5YB

* WISE WORDS * *

'WHAT IS A WORKING DAY?'

KARL MARX—(Das Kapital)

THE ADVENTUROUS WAY ROUND

MAKE WAY! We are the adventurous! And we're going on an adventure! We're going on an adventure around the world. Not for us the sour milk of mere existence! We sup only on the rich cream of experience! Make way! We're off to test our mettle, to see what we're made of. We're going on an adventurous round the world sort-the-men-from-the-boys, the wheat-from-the-chaff, the sheep-from-the-goats adventure.

Who knows what lies ahead? Who can tell how we'll fare? These are not matters that concern us. We're just going to roll up our sleeves, throw caution to the wind, grab life by the horns, feel the wind in our hair and head for the border. Yes, we'll be flying blind, by the seat of our pants, by the skin of our teeth, close to the wind, into the eye of the storm, under the radar, against all odds, but that's how we like it! Give us the raw flesh of vitality over the feeble salad bar of conformity any day! Make way! We're going on a hell for leather, all terrain, cross continent, full throttle whirlwind of reckless free-wheeling adventure!

We've got advisers, obviously. I mean, we're hell-for-leather, go-getting, frontier-pushing, out on a limb danger whores, not paperwork jockeys! We've got bigger fish to fry, taller mountains to cross, wider streams to ford. If someone offers to secure a few visas, book a few flights, arrange a few transfers, who are we to say no? Did Edmund Hillary knit his own ropes? Did Scott of the Antarctic breed his own huskies? Let others spend their time dabbing their clean-shaven chins with the tepid aftershaves of detail and drudgery—for us it's the great bushy beards of spontaneity! Make way!

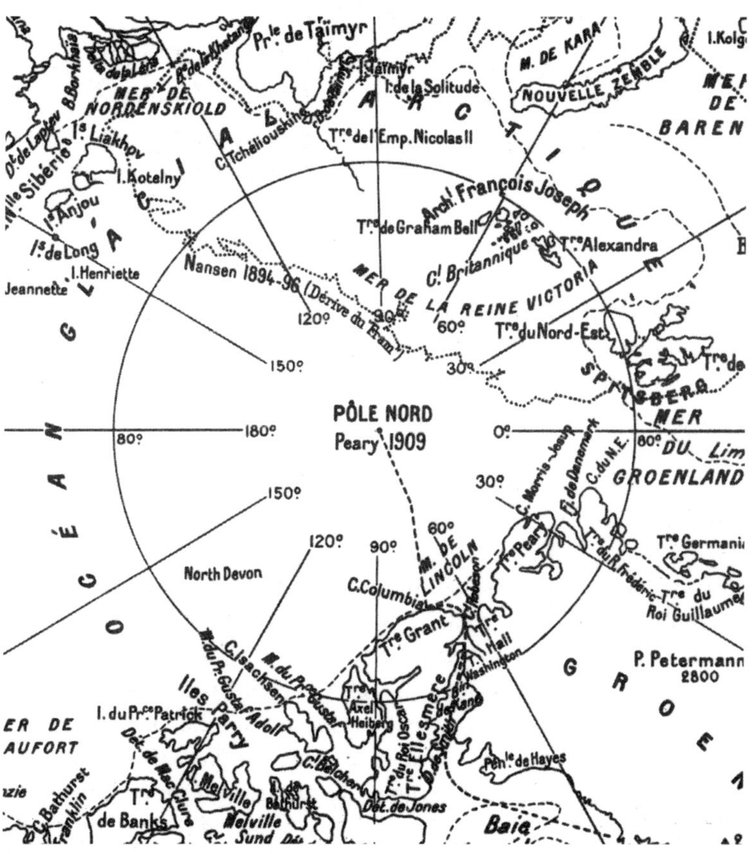

Although if we happen to be able to procure a linguist, say, to give us a few pointers on a selection of the local dialects, who are we to say no, non, nieta, ni, nahna? Obviously, we're wheelie-pulling, bear-hugging, life-affirming experience leeches, but we're not going to look mouthwards, gift-horse wise.

Ditto, of course, the medical specialists. It goes without saying that we're rock 'n' roll, no-holds barred, life-less ordinary living continent straddling thrill-fetchers, but we're not lunatics! Twenty four hour medical assistance isn't the sort of thing you can just turn down! Just think—we're entering the valley of the shadow of the jaws of the unknown once in a lifetime feel the fear and do it anyway adventurous adventure here, you think we want to risk all that being de-railed by having, say, an ingrown toenail go septic? No we do not! We just want to be able to get the thing fixed up and carry on! Who has time for such trifles, when adventure is to be had? Not us! Make way!

And if you think the satellite tracking, the driver, a mechanic, two minders and a small team of chefs is in any way incompatible with being a reach for the stars, touching the void, high rolling adrenaline chaser, then my friend you clearly don't know much about adventure! Keep both hands free at all times, to grab life round its shapely waist, throw it across your knee, and kiss it deeply on the mouth! You think when the chips are down, the stakes are high, the odds are against us, there'll be time for making sandwiches, quibbling over left or right, chatting to locals hassling us for coins or wanting to show us their smelly homes?

Camera crew, Corporate sponsorship consultants, financial advisers, stylists, media negotiators, publishing assistants, merchandising licensers, IT trouble-shooters, nutritional schedulers, armed response units, helicopter gunships at all times surveying the terrain from 4000 feet: You're seriously telling me you'd go anywhere at all without these firmly in place?

What are you, a psychopath with a raging death wish?

NICHOLAS PARKER *(Hatcham)*

Up for it?

Some Questions for Discussion

. 1 .
The different ideas we form of men
whose pursuit is money, power, distinction,
domestic happiness, public good.

. 2 .
Should we be led?

. 3 .
On what grounds may the forms,
ceremonies and restraints of polite society be objected to?
What purpose are they intended to answer?

. 4 .
Explain the phrases – 'a man of business',
'a man of pleasure', 'a man of the world'.

. 5 .
It is an oversight, surely, that in a society organised around the free
movement of capital, labour is not equally free?

. 6 .
The ways in which a man's style may be said
to offend against simplicity.

. 7 .
The love of stories, real or fabulous, in young and old.
Account for it, and what good use it may serve.

. 8 .
When the public fails in its duty,
what then?

. 9 .
What is the meaning of 'Fate',
in the ancient use of the word?
What is its popular signification now?

. 10 .
All men are mortal.

. 11 .
How many people exactly said they were unhappy with the way it was before?

. 12 .
Compare some of the methods of gaining or exercising Public Influence: as, Lectures, the Pulpit, Associations, The Press, Political Office.

. 13 .
An affront to democracy.

. 14 .
'The thunder's roar, the Lightning's flash, the billows' roar, the earthquakes' shock, all derive their dread sublimity from death.' Examine this theory.

. 15 .
Whether moral excellence tends directly to increase intellectual power?

. 16 .
Whither moral excellence?

. 17 .
The mark or standard by which a nation is judged to be barbarous or civilised. Barbarities of civilised states.

. 18 .
The commercial spirit of modern times considered in its influence on the Political, Moral, and Literary character of a Nation.

. 19 .
Nothing valuable can be marketed.

. 20 .
New Labour.

Compiled by: TONY GREEN *(Ipswich)*, J. STREET *(Felixstowe)*, DESMOND HAGLEY *(Hereford)*

Completely lost sight of your ethic?

theenthusiast@theenthusiast.co.uk
THE ENTHUSIAST, PO BOX 239, BANGOR, BT20 5YB

- WHAT I NEED -

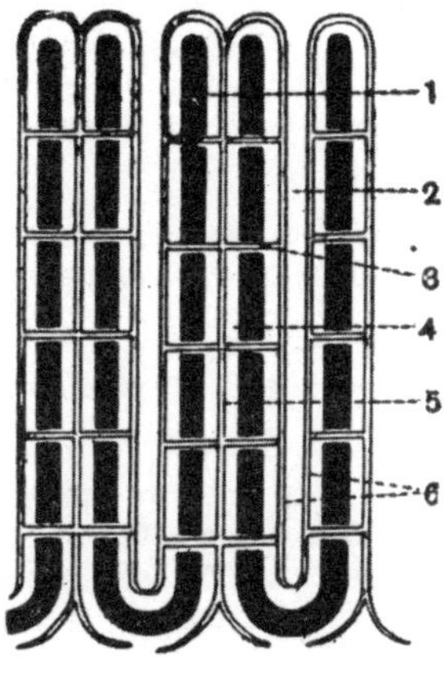

I need some kind of storage system.

BEVERLY ROSS *(Beverley)*

- HOME AND GARDEN -

How to Live

PLAN OF THE GALLERY

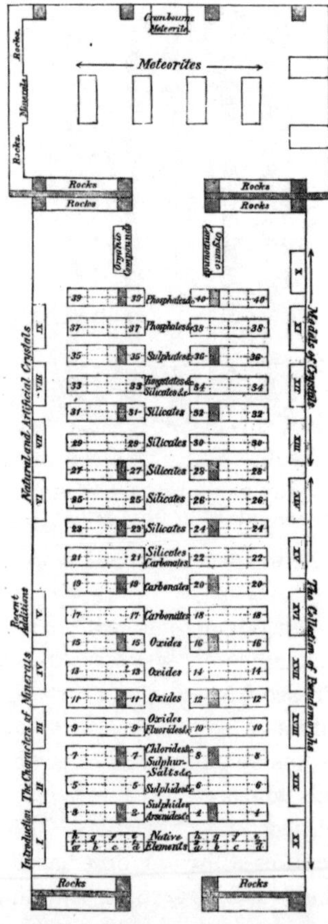

MOST 'PRIMITIVE SOCIETIES', lacking the sophisticated encumbrances of concert halls, museums, churches and so on, treat the house as the primary form of symbolic building. *The typical symbolism goes something like this : basement/earth is the past, often the burial ground for ancestors; the attic or roof is the head, the conscious part, and also a representation of the cosmos. Because we're all pretty much in the same soup cosmically speaking, such huts tend to look alike. Adventurous individual concepts of interior design are surplus to requirements.*

If you look at our typical hut—in the popular Barratt or Wimpey style, cod-nostalgic, pseudo-picturesque, individual identity assured by tiny changes in poor façade details between houses—it becomes clear that we are, in fact, sub-primitive as a society. We are spiritual plankton. We can't dwell. Our attics are inaccessible because the builders make more money using light prefab roof trusses which don't allow standing room. We fuck, fight, grow up, eat, shit, wash, sleep, dream, grow old and die in spaces that are moronically repetitive and bereft of meaning.

The recent property boom has made shelter (even of this depressing kind) an unattainable consumer luxury for most younger Britons, prompting Prescott and Blair to threaten Pharaonic Thames Gateway developments as a palliative. The quality of life they can offer should be treated as a major political issue, as it will outlive by generations the officials who launch the projects. But you can't blame *everything* on the politicos and developers. We have lost a shared cosmogony : our conception of the universe has more to do with navel-gazing than star-gazing. Our search for dwelling, for a place in the world, for our dream house, has become an enterprise of self-actualisation, working out in bricks and mortar what is worked out in words on the psychiatrist's couch.

Only a psychiatrist as barmy as Carl Jung would have the good grace (for the sake of my story) to have tried this exercise out for himself. He built and carved with his own hands a confabulation of stone huts on the shores of Lake Zurich, replete with his personal myth-map of cosmic worms, maternal forces and the like. He spoke of his dwelling as if it were an extension of his flesh, and vital to his identity.

For less self-assured members of society, you will need to recruit a new member to your family in order to realise your dream house : an architect. Filarete, the fifteenth-century architect and thinker, described the process thus : the client impregnates the architect with money, then nine months later a small relief model is born, which grows up under the joint tutelage of client and designer into a full-sized building. As we architects arrive with psychological and aesthetic baggage of our own, this process is never simple. In fact, having been through and observed it, I always see the hard, sure, certain, finished forms one sees in the architectural press and design books as obscenely fixed compared with the messy, uncertain process that always underlies their production.

I'd like to flesh out those cold images you see in *Architectural Digest* : what are the real stories underlying great buildings, what nightmares can one unleash through the process of creating a double-portrait in bricks and mortar of a client and creator?

Everything, in fact, depends on the quality of relationship between architect and patron. In general, the more supine the client, the more bizarre the built results will be. New York avant-gardist Peter Eisenman designed a series of doctrinaire houses early in his career which were named not after their clients but as a numerical series (thus underlining their creative paternity, their belonging to *his* family). Number VI was designed for Suzanne and Dick Frank, who gave him exceptionally free range. He put up a column obstructing the dining-room table, and made a glass slot which cut the marital bed in two. Alienation, I suppose. I presented the house to a conference of the French Family Psychotherapists' Association : they chortled (actually more of a *hur-hur*, as only the French can) when I showed a slide of Eisenman with his hand rather affectionately posed on the head of Suzanne Frank. They diagnosed the house as schizoid. The Franks had to restore the house after thirteen years (it was badly built) ; they bridged the slot and reunited the halves of their bed in the process. Eisenman claimed it lost its edge.

Frank Lloyd Wright went further than Eisenman may have done, running off with a client's wife, Mamah Borthwick Cheney. His own gaff, Taliesin (a sprawling farm-compound in Wisconsin) was run as a quasi-mystical commune, only a hair's breadth away from Branch Davidian bonkers. Students would travel from around the world to work (for free) in the master's studio, and find themselves milking cows instead. Frank held dinner with twelve guests every night, and guess who broke the bread ... Mamah Borthwick was unfortunately chopped up with an axe by Taliesin's butler, who then burned the place down.

Lloyd Wright was—philandering, exploitation and mumbo-jumbo aside—a genius, and his best houses arose from relationships of hysterical intensity with the clients. Fallingwater, his masterpiece, a series of improbably floating concrete shelves angled out over a waterfall, was born, quite appropriately, from a relationship of brinksmanship with client Edgar Kaufmann, each party threatening to abandon the project whenever their respective authority was impugned. The house plays on primal feelings : it's a sort of flying cave ; the bedrooms dark and earthy, seemingly incised in the rock, giving on to floating terraces which project one into the lush nature of the Bear Run valley. The Kaufmanns used the house for weekends very briefly, then decamped to a sunnier Richard Neutra house in Palm Springs. Fallingwater left a profound mark on their son Edgar Jr. (interestingly, an only child) who became an important architectural historian, and loved the place until his death.

Part of the problem of the dream house is that it is inevitably a skewed portrait of the inhabiting family. Children can't give orders to builders, but their need to settle, to feel appropriately clothed by their surroundings, is no less important than that of their parents, who are the ones in charge (or, most likely, the *one* in charge, Daddy). Fallingwater is upside-down compared to the norm, the child becoming the real dweller. More often than not the dream house becomes tainted psychological baggage, a mixed blessing and burden for the children to inherit and shoulder. This is often due to the fact that, if the house is particularly good, lots of other people feel that it is theirs. I have shimmied up walls and perched on precipitous fences just to

FIG. 74
Diagram of successive stages in the progress of a seal. 1, at rest. 2, 3, hind part of body arched and hind limbs drawn forward. 4, fore part of body raised on flippers and pushed forward by hind end. 5, fore part again on ground. 6, repeat

catch a glimpse of Maison X or Villa Y, doubtless much to the chagrin of their inhabitants. I'm sorry, by the way, but I just can't help it. And why oh why did you have to add that carport to House Z..........?

The exquisite Maison de Verre in Paris is a case in point. Dr Dalsace, the original client, commissioned an unusual live/work combo (a family house incorporating his gynaecological practice) from pioneer modernist Pierre Chareau. The hygienic atmosphere of the medical study permeates the living spaces of the house : then-innovative materials such as rubber tile flooring, as well as austere metal fittings, are carried throughout the building, and there is a delicate play of public and private, with pivoting screens and eye-height frosted-glass partitions dividing the house as if it were a piece of machinery unfolding around an elaborate dance. The dance is carried through to Monsieur and Madame's bathroom, which they could rearrange with aluminium screens and folding wardrobes according to how much of each other they wanted to see. Dalsace loved the building deeply, a fact which frustrated his children, as a rather heavy, venerative atmosphere prevailed : no football in the living room, it might dent those divine perforated metal screens on the bookshelves ; steady on the stairs, junior, there's no guard rail. The kids left the house, and allow it to be seen by those willing to submit themselves to arcane membership and visiting rules. They each keep a room there, nonetheless, and one daughter married a gynaecologist herself (as you do), who practised in his father-in-law's cabinet until his retirement a couple of years ago, keeping the torture-chamber-grade 1920s equipment.

Le Corbusier dedicated his life, so he said, to an attempt to re-infuse the dwelling with a sense of the spiritual. He carried this out at the scale of large collective dwellings (like his controversial Unité d'Habitation in Marseille) and a series of private houses which rank as some of the most significant buildings of the last hundred years. Some were a tad rhetorical : his early Villa Savoye, a white prism on stilts in a field outside Paris, looks out of place, yearning to toddle on its piloti to a rugged spot overlooking the Med, bathed in sunlight rather than drenched in northern damp. The clients left it quite quickly, and then it was a hay store during the war. Now it has found its true vocation as a pure museum space with a bit of Corb furniture thrown in. The building needs its vast original site ; but urban expansion led to the construction of a blue high school looming over the house, destroying its core qualities of infinite prospect and abstract isolation. The high school is named 'Le Corbusier'.

Two other of his houses near Paris are far more personal and modest, and their destiny has been closely linked to the unusual family structure of their initial client. André Jaoul was a wealthy industrialist and art collector ; he decided to build twin houses, one for himself and his wife, and one for his son and young family. Le Corbusier conceived them as a fragment of a city, arranged at right angles with a miniature piazza between them. The houses were built of rugged bricks (the brickies were moved around the site at half-hour intervals to avoid homogeneity in the finish), plus roughcast concrete and wood. They have a primitive air, and are similar in appearance, declining their system of vaulted floor construction differently as if they were related pieces of music in the same key. The harmony was soon broken : Jaoul père died before the buildings' completion in 1954.

Michel Jaoul (the son) lived on with his widowed mother rattling around alone in the vast senior house. Feeling out of scale with the double character of the houses (his own children had moved on and his wife was infirm), he sold them in 1987 but continues to live on the same street, visiting occasionally. The buyer was Peter Palumbo, an avid collector of houses (he also owns a Frank Lloyd Wright pad near Fallingwater and Mies van der Rohe's glassy Farnsworth House built in a swamp outside Chicago ; Mies' refusal to install insect screens—they would destroy the transparency—apparently led the original owner literally to develop a thicker skin once the mosquitoes had had their way with him). Palumbo loved the Maisons Jaoul, restoring them with the original builders, all brought out of retirement for one last job. He kept one house for himself and generously allowed visits to the second. Palumbo had the means to keep the houses going, and during his residency they really felt like homes—warm, welcoming, well furnished and decorated. Unfortunately he had to sell up after a dispute with his family trust (there are rumours that he was in conflict with his son James, who removed all the trust-owned furniture from the houses one day). Now they are owned by two sisters, who didn't particularly like the architecture but were enchanted by the possibility of having two houses together in Neuilly-sur-Seine. Perhaps the Maisons Jaoul have found their destiny finally in the unlikeliest of ways.

Le Corbusier's best domestic clients (because they were close to his own outlook on life) were the Dominican brothers of his La Tourette Monastery. This is a hair-shirt building, a tough, all-concrete fortress where the various rough surfaces catch the slowly changing light of the monk's ordered day, making time act like a drug. One of the brothers confessed to me that whenever he returns from his frequent trips abroad, he is happy (and slightly surprised) to see the building still there, and caresses its columns, seeing it as something soft, delicate and loving.

Corb was similarly gruff when he built for himself : he had a functional apartment in Paris and a log cabin four metres square perched on the Mediterranean seashore where, amazingly, he and his wife stayed for a month every year. He died swimming in the sea by this house. He also built a charming and austere one-room dwelling for his parents by the shore of Lake Geneva. His father, a successful

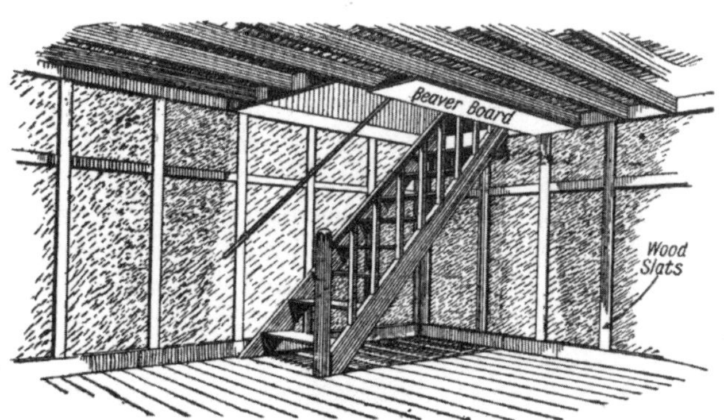

Coal Cellar. Method of converting a coal cellar into a useful room

journalist and publisher, had grown tired of the damp and cold of La Chaux de Fonds in the Jura (he had perhaps also grown tired of the slightly bombastic villa his adolescent son had designed for the couple). He died within a year of retiring to the warmer climes of Montreux, but his wife lived until a hundred, claiming she prayed every day not to suffer the sin of pride for having brought into the world its greatest architect. Corb survived her by only six years.

He and his wife, Yvonne, built another tiny shack attached to the house (two bunk beds, a desk by a window, access by ladder) for their visits as they themselves became old.

The shed or hut is the degree zero of the dream house : minimum comfort, minimum fuss, existenz minimum. Writers (Dylan Thomas, famously) have been particularly fond of sheds for the isolated, freestanding concentration they afford. In a shed one approximates the condition of Adam, the first dweller, who, Joseph Rykwert posits in his book *On Adam's House in Paradise*, must have had a hut (where else do you store the Edenic fruit and veg?). We can yearn, but at the end of the day we are outcasts, bound to imperfection, confined by what Henry James called our individual 'terrible algebra' as we seek our place in the world. Filarete showed this in his beautiful drawing of the expelled Adam forming a roof above his head with his hands to protect him from the elements : surely the first low-cost self-build. Let's hope this doesn't give Prescott and Blair any ideas.

ANDREW TODD *(Paris)*

LIVES OF THE FAMOUS

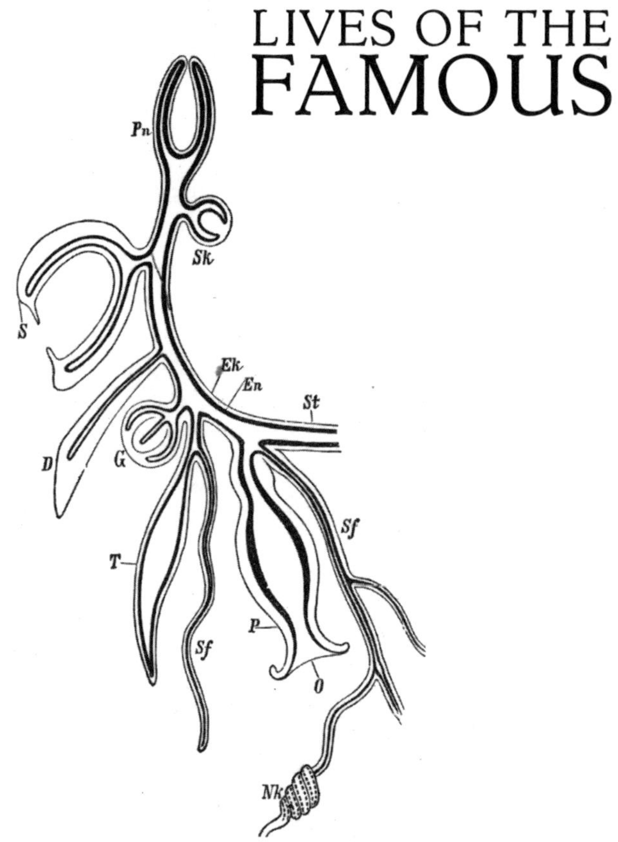

WILLIAM CARLOS WILLIAMS—William Carlos Williams was a student at the University of Pennsylvania. Fed up with hearing piano music from the room next door, Williams picked up his fiddle and started playing loudly in response. His piano-playing neighbour, hearing the music, introduced himself and they became friends. The piano-player introduced Williams to a young poet called Ezra Pound.

BETTY WARNE *(Liverpool)*

Klezmer? Serialism?

theenthusiast@theenthusiast.co.uk THE ENTHUSIAST, PO BOX 239, BANGOR, BT20 5YB

THE MOUSE OF THOUGHT—

I want to give up factory-farming. I want to go organic. I want to get my teeth fixed. I want to be able to buy a nice bespoke suit. I know I can. There's no reason why I can't. I know people can change their lives. Look at Yusif Islam, or Sammy Davis Jnr., or Shirley Temple. Pete Best–he's not a good example, obviously. But Samuel Beckett–in 1931 Samuel Beckett realised that he didn't want to be a Professor, and he'd already written a book on Proust and was teaching French at TCD at the time. Cary Grant started out life as a stilt-walker at Coney Island. Jackson Pollock was a lumberjack. And Bertrand Russell used to run a sea-food stall outside a pub in Leyton-stone. I know, I know, I know. I must change my life.

- HEALTH -

HOW TO BREATHE

Single-cell organisms can exchange oxygen and carbon dioxide directly with the external environment (the world), but this is obviously impossible for most cells of a complex organism like the human body ; most cells of a complex organism like the human body being tucked away, discreetly, from sight. In order to survive, large animals (the elephant would be an example of a large animal) have had to develop specialised systems for the supply of oxygen and the elimination of carbon dioxide. These systems are not the same in all complex animals—in the case of the elephant what we're clearly talking about here is the trunk—since evolution often follows several pathways simultaneously. We call these pathways bio-diversity. [Excellent.] The organs of gas exchange with the external environment (the world) in fish are gills ; those in man are lungs.

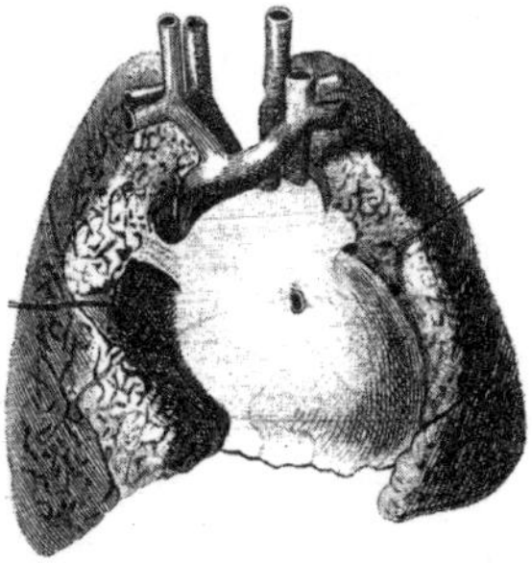

In a man or woman at rest, the body's cells consume approximately 200 ml of oxygen per minute. This is a lot. Under conditions of severe oxygen requirement—like when you're exercising, making love, fitting silently in a darkened room—the rate of oxygen consumption may increase as much as thirty-fold. Equivalent amounts of carbon dioxide are simultaneously eliminated. It is obvious, therefore, that mechanisms must exist which coordinate breathing with metabolic demands. We can call this mechanism the respiratory system.

The term respiratory system refers only to those structures which are involved in the exchange of gases between the blood and the external environment (the world). Oxygen has to be absorbed into the blood because the body depends on it. Carbon dioxide has to go out into the world because, frankly, there is nowhere else for it to go. The respiratory system comprises the lungs, the series of passageways leading to the lungs, and the chest structures responsible for movement of air in and out of the lungs.

[You might, at this point, like to think about your own breathing for a moment. Is it steady? Can you rely on it? Are your chest structures as responsive as they might be? Are your passageways clear? Are you lungs capacious? Do you exchange successfully with the world?]

We press on.

In order for air to reach the lungs, it must first pass through a series of air passages connecting the lungs to the mouth. There are two lungs, the right and the left, each divided into several lobes. Together with the heart, great vessels, oesophagus, and certain nerves, the lungs completely fill the *chest (thoracic) cavity*. Nor are the lungs simply hollow balloons—the hollow balloon is the wrong analogy—but have themselves a highly organised structure : air-containing tubes, blood vessels, elastic connective tissue. The air passages within the lungs are the continuation of those which connect the lungs to the nose and the mouth. This is where the world comes in. Together we will call these tubes the *conducting tubes* of the respiratory system. These tubes branch, and as they branch so they become smaller, and as they branch so they become more numerous, more numerous even than it is comfortable to imagine, the very smallest ending in tiny blind sacs. And it is here, in these tiny, sightless arenas that the exchange of gases actually occurs. We call these sacs the alveoli. Everything tends towards the alveoli.

Air.

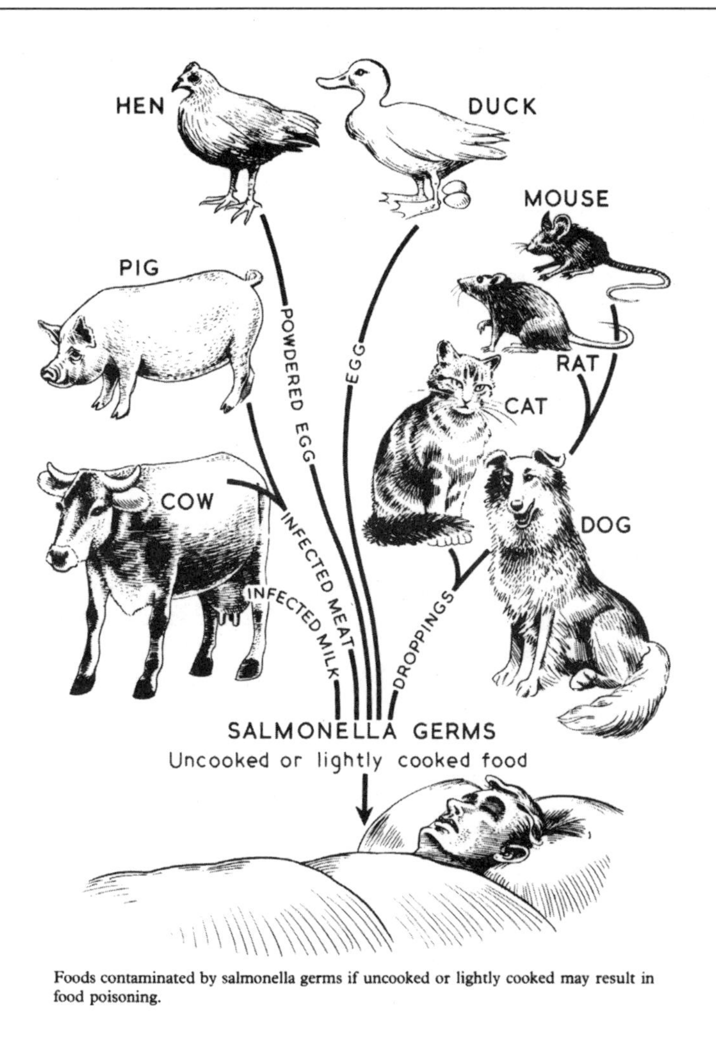

Foods contaminated by salmonella germs if uncooked or lightly cooked may result in food poisoning.

Air can.

Air can enter.

Air can enter the respiratory passages either by the nose or mouth. The nose is good if you are eating, and is, anyway, the more conventional route. It [the air] then passes into the *pharynx* (throat), a passage common to the routes followed by air and food. The pharynx branches—*the pharynx branches*!—into two tubes, one (the *oesophagus*) through which food passes into the stomach and one through which air passes into the lungs. We won't now here follow the food into the stomach, but will, with the air, press on down into the lungs. Down : the first portion of the air passage, called the *larynx*, houses the vocal cords ; those two strong bands of elastic tissue, which stretch across the lumen of the larynx ; strong enough to prevent the lungs filling with food. The movement past them of air causes them to vibrate, initiating the many different sounds which constitute speech. For instance, 'Lumen', 'Larynx', 'Lungs', 'Oesophagus', 'Heart', 'Nerves', 'Alveoli'.

To conclude, breathing consists of an *exchange of air between the atmosphere* (the world) *and the alveoli*. This process includes the movement of air in and out of the lungs and the distribution of air within the lungs. Not only must a large volume of new air be delivered constantly to the alveoli (those unseeing sacs, sightless sites of exchange) but it must be distributed evenly to the millions of alveoli within each lung. Each single alveoli filling with each inspiration. We call this process ventilation.

There is more to breathing, more one could dwell on : the exchange of oxygen and carbon dioxide between air and lung capillaries by diffusion ; the transportation of oxygen and carbon dioxide by the blood ; the exchange of oxygen and carbon dioxide between the blood and tissues of the blood by diffusion as blood flows through tissue capillaries. Imagine it, though, millions of alveoli, simultaneously filling up.

In. Out.

In. Out.

We call this process ventilation.

Puffed?

theenthusiast@theenthusiast.co.uk

THE ENTHUSIAST, PO BOX 239, BANGOR, BT20 5YB

Ab-

An Appreciation.

So there we were, all bedded down in prefixes, our *ante*-s and *anti*-s, your *post*-, his *pre*-, *a*-, *an*-, *un*- and her glorious *ultra*- when the issue arose. Was it not an abuse, an abnegation of our troth, this abjection of the abjunctive wonder of *ab*-? It is sap (to be absorbed) to be sure. It is more than the fifth month of the Hebrew year (eleventh of the civil year, twelfth of the Syrian year, that which answers to August) though surely, that is more than most letter pairings can hope for (even noble Xu is only one-hundredth of a Dong).

Outdone once upon a time only by *ou*-, not 'ou' compounded and echoed as in Ougadougou, but standing proudly alone and as a remarkable sixteenth century prefix (*ou*-, ah, glory days indeed, my friends, glory days indeed), *ab*- is as close as the keen abecedarian needs to get to literacy to touch upon a lodestone of lexical reverence.

Gazing upon this unassuming morpheme, one mourns the day it birthed the ubiquitous and déclassé *a*-. But we choose to ablaqueate and lift *ab*-, that we may enjoy it as new. Abjugated from the bulky abdomen of the signification, ablacted from its modificand, this diminutive prefix finds its aboriginal pragnanz in the simplicity of 'off', 'away', 'from'. The chill in my feet alerted me to the fact that we had lingered too long with *ab*-. Bound to it as I was, I was to be the abactor of our communion. I roused her from her contemplation gently so as not to abalienate her and we performed our ablution in quiet reverence, climbing the foothills to reach the skyline where *de*- waited quietly. It suited her grace to be indulgent of our veneration of her cousin *ab*-. She could do no less, and neither could we.

JOSH BROWN *(Brighton)*

Swallowed a dictionary?

Antifascist Risotto

CREDIT FOR THE RECIPE should go to my friend Toni Vianello, whose restaurant in the Rue de S---- is an omphalos of fine living, a secret gathering-point for those who share an overweening need for the highest quality presented in an informal manner, something which is actually much easier than you think.

This recipe serves six: you will need 400 to 550g of rice, depending on whether you plan to add other ingredients (meat, veg, it's up to you). The rice should be Arborio or Carnaroli. Cook a finely-chopped medium onion in two tablespoons of olive oil, medium heat, don't let it brown. After 10–12 minutes, when the onion should be slightly translucent, add the rice and stir gently but thoroughly, impregnating it with the oil. The grains should take on a certain translucence, but on no account a brownish tinge which would mean their protein envelope was destroyed, allowing the vital amidon contained within to leach. Add wine (generally white, but can be champagne or red depending on what you plan to add in terms of meat and/or veg), enough to moisturise all the rice (between half a glass and a glass), allow to evaporate completely. Add one and a half litres of stock. You must make this stock yourself from the finest ingredients, otherwise it's just not worth the bother. This, again, is much easier than you think. Then – and this is the key to the ethos implied above – cover the pot, turn down to low heat and LEAVE ALONE FOR TWELVE MINUTES. I'm not going to enter into any polemics on this subject; I've paid my dues, my lower spine remembers hours of Elizabeth David-induced splosh-stir, splosh-stir anxiety, needless husbandry bent over the stove. You'll just have to believe me and try for yourselves. And think what you can do with those twelve minutes: meditate, make love, listen to certain longer movements of Beethoven's symphonies, read the shorter among the short of Beckett's short plays. Over the course of years this will add up to countless hours of your life regained.

Recipe to share?

theenthusiast@theenthusiast.co.uk

The Enthusiast, PO Box 239,
BANGOR BT20 5YB

You finish by adding whatever extra bits you desire (cooked asparagus, funghi porcini, roast pheasant), cook for a further three to four minutes, check the seasoning, add 80g of cold butter and 80g of freshly grated parmesan (pronounced parme-*zan*, and not as the Americans prefer *parmezjan*, as in Azerbaidjan; it's not zjan but zan, as in courtesan; where the san is as in Zanzibar; it would be an error to suppose the zan is as San Juan). Then you leave the concoction two minutes off the heat, then and only then mix in vigourously the cheese and butter with a wooden fork. You can also add parsley, but this must be your call. Serve immediately. With friends.

ANDREW TODD *(Paris)*

– WHAT I NEED –

I need some more time
to be an individual in.

CURTIS WESTWOOD *(Nebraska)*

Me time?

* WISE WORDS * *

'1. THE SLIM RECOGNISE EACH OTHER.
2. THE CRUSTED DO NOT RECOGNISE THE SLIM.'

ANDRÉ GIDE—(The Vatican Cellars)

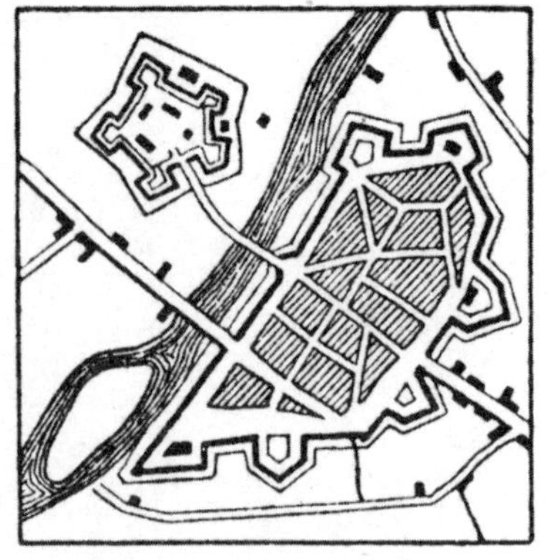

Retranch, Redoutes

Ville ouverte

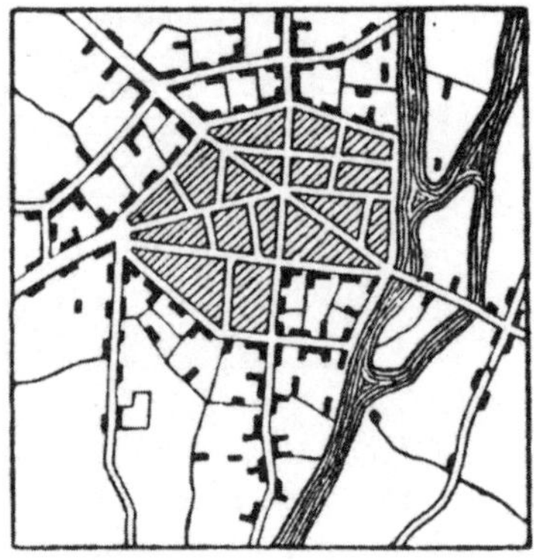

Port de mer

Bourg ou village

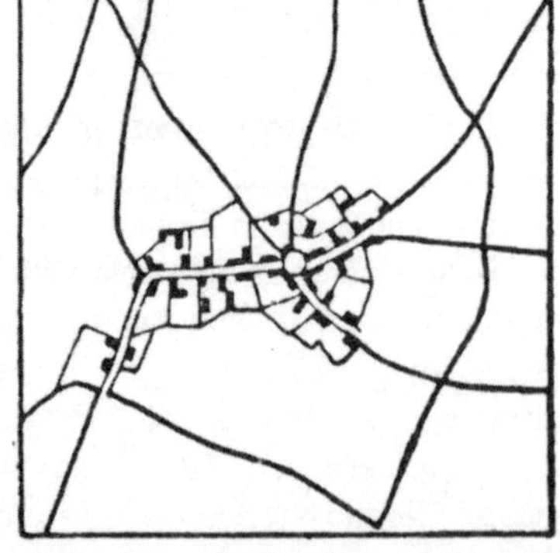

- TRAVEL -

INDIA:

A Rough Guide

If you already happen to have a plum view of sheep, or the sea, or your local tobacconist, I can understand why you might find the very idea of travel quite unnecessary.

ALL THE SAME, I would still firmly encourage you to do it, as early as you can, for very soon travel will no longer be possible. Allow me to explain. You will have noticed, no doubt, that you have been living for longer than you expected to. Today you are much more likely to die at the age of ninety than seventy. In fact, thanks to recent and upcoming advances in our technology, you will soon be slogging on with absolutely no end in sight—that is, by virtue of either upload or download, you will be immortal. Concomitant to this, other recent advances in our technology have made it much easier to go from one place to another and also be in several places at the same time. Very soon, you will be in so many places at the same time that you will no longer be sure of where you are. This may lead to some amount of anxiety when, as you are having your ten billionth cup of coffee on the afternoon of your 233rd birthday, you find yourself unable to do anything, because it has already been done, or go anywhere, because you are already there. Luckily for you, the right to suicide will by then have been enshrined as a universal and inalienable human right, and thanks to even more advances in our technology, killing yourself, far from being the cumbersome and unreliable process it is today, will have become as simple as turning off your television set. However, if you choose not to exercise that right, then you might wish you had *travelled*, at a younger age, so that you could now amuse yourself by making up memories about it.

There it is. And while I would not want to be so bold as to suggest where you might travel to, may I offer my own native place, India and the Golden Chersonese, not to mention the utmost Indian isle, Taprobane? This is because, for reasons related to those above, according to the predictions of our Ministry of Disinvestment, India will only exist, at the very latest, until about 2013. You will have noticed, no doubt, that India has, in the past ten years or so, been moving quietly and swiftly towards you. Already it is far closer to you than Libya or, for that matter, Burnley. In a matter of months even, it may have reached your nearest T-junction, and thereafter it may be a matter of days or even hours, before you are no longer able to depart from England to India or vice versa. At that moment, by a slight but inexorable hinge of perception, both states will disappear for ever. And not long after that, the only places it will still be possible to travel to will be Borneo (perhaps), Burnley, and possibly Uranus. But fear not! India is still here (or there) for now, and if you travel to India this summer, you will still be able to witness the exotic sight of men casually opening the doors of their SUVs at traffic lights to lean out and spit a thick wad's worth of *betel-nut juice* on the road ; and in general, you will be able to see and collect an astounding number of those very minute, fractional differences in habitation, habitability and *habitus* that continue to make travel such a rewarding, much discussed and popular experience. Here then, are some suggestions and tips for your visit:

Baths. By all means, please do have them. This may sound like self-evident advice, but it is remarkable how many travellers from the West—a High Street banker, for instance, or a certain professor of Classics at Oxford who shall go unnamed—who would normally be very scrubbed and scented in their natural environments, decide to go unwashed in India and sport the look of grubby vagabonds. Inexplicable, really, how such individuals fail to grasp, weeks or even months after their arrival, that there is no creature that the average Indian, regardless of class background, respects less than a dirty foreigner. You may decide not to bathe in the interests of saving the environment ; but deciding to save the environment right on your arrival in India may be something akin to suddenly turning into a militant vegan on your arrival in Uzbekistan : not recommended. Rather, *take baths* as a kind of incessant spiritual ablution, for how often have I been transformed, by just three-quarters of a bucket of water and a sliver of soap, from a half-grovelling, half-cussing *pie-dog* into a softly blubbering infant, poof in the midst of a gruelling summer evening in North India! There is no greater redemption. Furthermore, I would insist that a bath in India has more shamanic power than almost anywhere else in the world, and I am a well-travelled gentleman myself. (Of course, I did once have a particularly divine bath at the home of a lovely lady editor in Whitstable, but that was for other reasons as well, and in the end, was only the exception that proved the rule.)

As a rule of thumb, then, begin by taking five baths a day : one on waking, one before lunch, one before shopping, one after shopping, and one just before sleep. Thereafter, take more baths as needed or desired, but be sure to cap the number of your daily baths at nine. If you find yourself taking baths in the double figures, consult a doctor immediately. You are showing signs of obsessive-compulsive behaviour and this may mean that the bacterium *Salmonella typhi* that you accidentally imbibed on one of your many baths, after having done some of its own travelling in and out of your intestines, has now comfortably ensconced itself in the folds of your cranial tissue. In general, the main trick with water is to recognise its different varieties, and to apprehend which kind of water goes in where.

Clothing. You may wish to saunter about in one of the various varieties of traditional costume, but this is not advised unless you have gauged exactly where along the sartorial continuum you ought to fall. You should be careful when attempting to emulate the model of Westerners familiar with India. You might, for instance, try to adopt the style of William Dalrymple, otherwise known in these parts as the White Mogul, with elaborate white *kurtas* and *Arabian Nights*-style pointy shoes, but then you might rapidly find yourself gathering and ministering to a coterie of third-rate sycophants ; being a White Mogul is, at any rate, only fun half the time. If you should choose to take on the Rousseau-meets-Gandhi-in-the-Ghetto style of French economist Jean Dreze, you might well be mistaken for a Maoist by the police, and shot at. In general, you should bear in mind that ethnic Cherie Blairism is not necessarily likely to win you the right kind of friends, except at high-society parties the world over. Ideally, wear designer T-shirts and jeans and flashy, branded sneakers ; Indians are very appreciative of this. Alternatively, a pith helmet and immaculately pressed safari suit, with socks pulled up to the knees might be out of style, but is still likely to attract a surprising amount of respect and deference.

Accommodation. On your arrival at Delhi airport, you will head straight for the area near the main railway station known as Paharganj. There you will find yourself a cheap room, and after that, you will stroll down to the Everest Café. At the café, for an hour, you will listen first to the woman they call the California Rose hold forth—in imprecise language—on her trysts with Indian *sadhus*, and later, a round of Israelis discussing dysentery. After two cups of *chai*, you will return to consider your lice-infested room and realise, in a moment of sudden clarity, that the room has been incalculably overpriced. At this point, you will gather your bags, call a cab, and proceed to check in at the Sheraton. You will stay at that Sheraton for the rest of your life.

Fig. 44.—Bed-rest.

—Improvised Bed rest.

Handy Phrases. Below, you will find a list of phrases in the local language. Do memorise and practise these carefully before your departure ; they have been chosen specifically with *The Enthusiast*'s readership in mind ; they will be of use to you in most parts of India. Translations of these phrases are unnecessary because they are equally applicable and relevant in all situations :

No, no, nahin! Mein American nahin hoon!

Ek Pepsi dedho, bhai-sahib.

Kya cool hai!

Yes, yes, bhilkul theek. Mein Italian hoon.

Kuch hashish milenga, bhai?

Koi baat nahin, asshole.

Jassi jaisi kohi nahin!

A.C. nahin chalega? Kya baat hai?

Pandara rupiah! Bas! Chalo! Fadaafat!

Hai! What to do? K.L.P.D.—Khade lund par dhoka, he he he he ...

Places to Visit : The Malls of Gurgaon. Massive malls designed like huge glass-fronted boxes, embedded with multiplex theatres, often designed in a slightly unique style that can only be described as Miami-meets-Nehruvian-chock-a-block, are a must for any visitor to the Indian city. Increasingly they can be found everywhere, but on the far outskirts of the big city they can be seen in small herds, interspersed with Egyptian-themed high-rise living complexes but surrounded by vast, as yet undeveloped grazing or dump land. Since, in places like Delhi, the idea of a completely artificial mini-city environment can be rather appealing at the height of summer, the malls are inhabited by entire extended families as opposed to angst-ridden teenagers.

Why bother with the Taj Mahal when these rather sturdy-looking monuments are liable to last even longer? In conjunction with the Metros and the new grand, spaghetti flyovers, they are part of a plan by the Ministry of Disinvestment to create a new well-secured India,

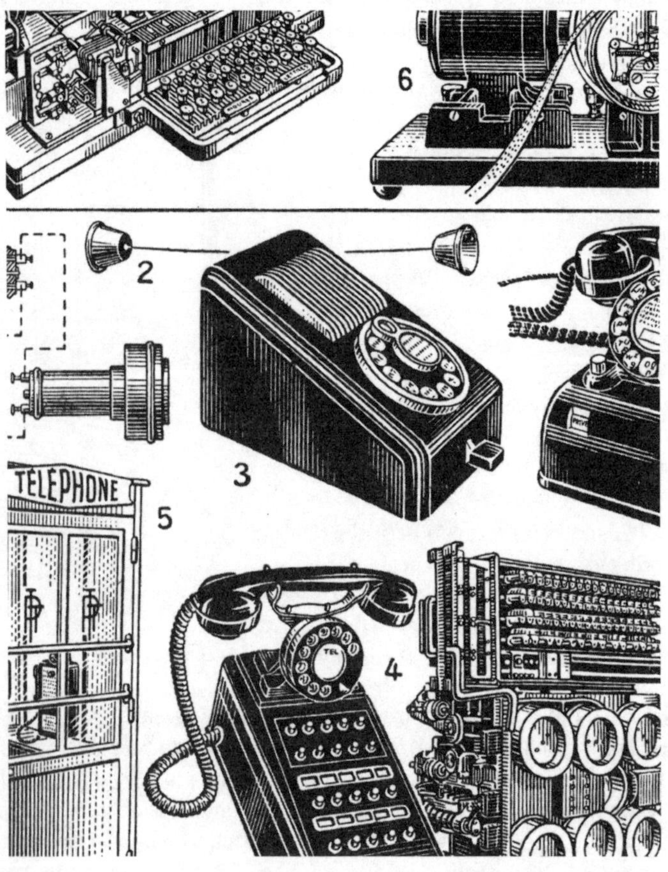

suspended a few hundred feet above the old one, where poverty, the anopheles mosquito, diesel smoke, heat, dirt, open-pit *latrines* and *betel-nut* spit will all be things of the past. Once the entire working city has been completed at this altitude, it will be carefully lowered with the use of hydraulic technology until it has supplanted any last construction left on the ground. You may ask, what about the poor?

But, no need to worry. That is hardly a relevant question in the current dispensation ; for, as the Ministry of Disinvestment assures us, every last roadside peanut-seller, feudal sharecropper, maid, rag-picker and bar-dancer will, by that time, have been transformed by the magic wand of development into suave, multi-faceted nuclear scientists, jive-talking software engineers or, at worst, jive-talking, Prada-wearing call-centre kids.

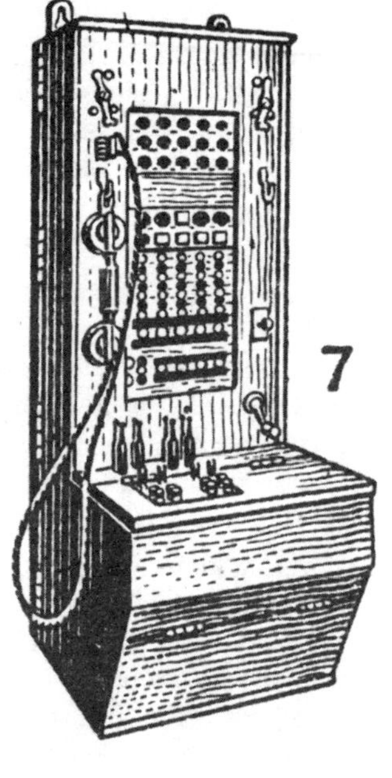

Other Things to See. The 'rural' Indian landscape, with miles of wide fields on either side of the road. A bull with a large nose-ring on which a produce-filled cart hangs. A tractor, not on the fields but on the delicate road heading towards a town, piled up with passengers on every available ledge, including children precarious on the bumpers above the front wheels, holding on to the vertical exhaust pipe for support.

A snatch of a town, with the deshabillé of rural construction, and people lined up in front of the blue, reliable touchstone of the State Bank of India. Hundreds and hundreds of flattened, brown packing cartons, some of them loaded on open-top *auto-rickshaws*. The two-lane highway which passes through this landscape, given massive traffic jams at 3 a.m. Set against the fields and the cheap, shabby *kurta pajamas* of those men who are walking towards the road, an impossibly large and slick billboard advertisement for a cellular phone company, intended to make those who are passing through this landscape feel at home.

Dhabas, or roadside restaurants, which are all called Godavari. Three young men hitching a ride on the back of a truck, holding on to the horizontal bar above them for support, and posing like potential movie stars.

Sound. As I type these words in at an *internet café*, I am flanked, just an inch or two from my elbow, by four men, strangers, sitting around in a loose circle, considering question papers or figures printed on accounting paper, looking occasionally over my shoulder to read part of what I am writing, and talking towards the top of their voice—completely oblivious, it would seem, to the fact that here I am trying to think out and write this short article of national importance. The AC hums shudderingly along, another customer watches cricket commentary on his screen without the use of headphones, and just beyond the computer cubicle, a clump of customers are losing their patience and arguing with the unfazed woman behind the desk. In other words, my immediate environment is reasonably quiet.

If, however, I were to step out into the street, this would change. I would be confronted with the multiple snorts of diesel trucks, the sudden commotion of a wedding band blocking the main road, the distorted, barely parsable, battling radios of two competing roadside shops, workers taking a massive pickaxe to concrete, and luxury sedans trying to horn a *cycle-rickshaw* off the road and a bus behind them bellowing back (vehicle horns in these latitudes being less emergency warnings than instruments of an extra language in which an entire range of rhythmic personal expression is breathlessly made use of)—all of this in one simultaneous and unbroken symphony.

The chances are that you are reading of this in a quieter place, which is part of what still keeps our two places apart. On arrival, you may take a little while to adjust to the acceptable urban Indian levels of immunity to sound, but you are advised not to use earplugs. Better to enjoy it to the hilt as if it were all part of one vast experimental music concert, clapping at the appropriate times ; for what more could an experimental music aficionado want, except that his life-changing concerts be unending?

Your Humble Correspondent

VIVEK NARAYANAN *(New Delhi)*

LIVES OF THE FAMOUS

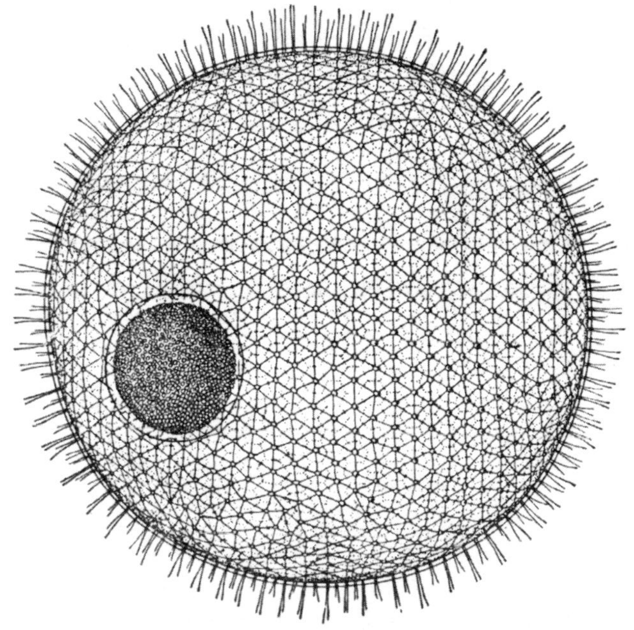

ERIK SATIE—*1)* I wear white socks and white vest, along with a velvet coat, soft felt hat and flowing tie (which is partially hidden by my beard), and on my nose I wear my pince-nez of course. *2)* My expression is very serious. When I laugh, it is unintentional and I always apologise, very politely. *3)* I breathe carefully (a little at a time), and dance very rarely. When walking, I hold my ribs and look steadily behind me. *4)* For a long time I have subscribed to a fashion magazine. *5)* My only nourishment consists of food that is white (I spare you the details for it sounds revolting). *6)* Before writing a work I walk around it several times accompanied by myself. *7)* My doctor has always told me to smoke (cigarettes of course). He even explains himself: 'Smoke, my friend. Otherwise someone else will smoke in your place.'

NICK PARKER *(Hatcham)*

Whimsicality standing in the way of widespread recognition?

theenthusiast@theenthusiast.co.uk THE ENTHUSIAST, PO BOX 239, BANGOR, BT20 5YB

FOR THEIR OWN SAFETY, MIDGETS ARE NOT ALLOWED ON THE RIDES.

IT'S ILLEGAL TO SLEEP UNDERGROUND.

YOU CAN'T TAKE BROWNIES OVER THE TREE-LINE.

- HEALTH -

HOW'S YOUR POSTURE?

WE LIVE IN SEDENTARY TIMES. As I write I am sitting in an orthopaedically approved office chair. It is anticipated that, with time, this will improve my posture, correct me, render me more upright—from the Greek *orthos* meaning straight, or straighten out. The chair is spring-loaded so that I can adjust myself to the height of my desk—or rather, to the height of the retractable keyboard shelf on my pine-effect workstation. The back of the chair tilts and can be fixed at the angle of my choice, the armrests swivel, and offer variable heights. The whole chair is on wheels, which sit at the end of five plastic spokes, so that if I push hard enough I can slide the length of my workroom to my window. On the roof outside a starling is serenading his mate. He is noted for his imitations. It is Valentine's Day after all.

You are sitting too. I like to think of you in the middle of a cinema, a small independent, before the lights go down, or at the back of a lecture hall, one ear on the speaker's progress, poised in case anything purposeful should be said ; on a bus, or on a train, or on a long, green leather bench, in a café in Bolton discussing the benefits of immigration, on a beach watching dolphins sport towards evening, in a pub with a friend recalling re-runs of Morecambe and Wise. Or maybe you're in a detention centre, or you're on a long-haul flight, or you're at the bar of an overnight cross-channel ferry, or you're in a queue, or a canteen, or you're sitting on the side of the mountain, on a park-bench maintained by a local authority franchise. I imagine you sitting there, unperturbed by details of the tender, contemplating crocuses. The chances are you're on a sofa.

Sitting can be good. Much has been achieved by the human seated. The Buddha, son of the king of Kapilavatsu (at the foot of the mountains of Nepal), finding salvation neither in the teaching nor in the austerities of the Brahmans, developed by long meditations his own religion, which he expounded in various places in India, making many disciples. Suffering, he preached, is inseparable from existence, which is an evil ; the principal cause of suffering is desire ; the suppression of suffering can be obtained by the suppression of desire. And so the Buddha sat, and has ever since been depicted sitting, serene in the face of worldly promptings. Kant sat also, and we are wise to sit with him. Karl Marx sat in the Reading Room of the British Museum. Lenin sat for a while and pondered 'What is to be done?' Socrates walked, asking questions as he went. Emily Dickinson sat. Emily Pankhurst stood. Philip Roth writes while standing. He composes at a lectern and paces the room restlessly between sentences. There are reasons to be suspicious of our seated self.

'To give light to them that sit in darkness and in the shadow of death, to guide our feet in the way of peace.' Luke, 1:79. And Luke is right, surely, that when we sit we do so in darkness, for in our sedentary self is our sedate self. It is by our feet and in their appropriate exercise that we make our way serenely towards the light.

Amen

There is, perhaps, an image in modern culture more obscene than that of the British Prime Minister seated on the couch chatting to camera with two fabulous personalities, whose capital is their representativeness which they communicate chiefly by their posture,

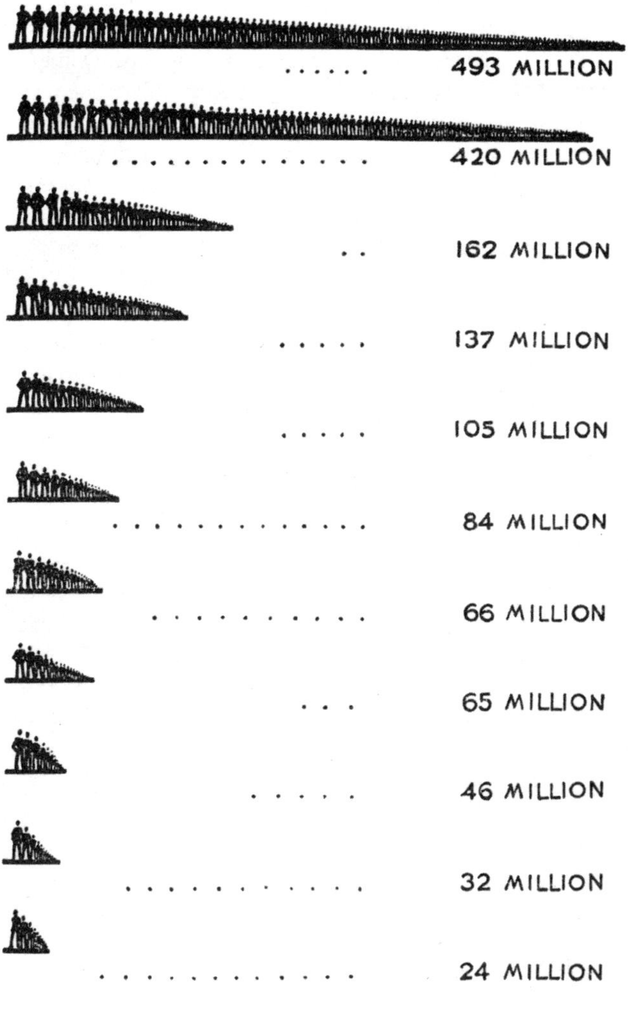

493 MILLION

420 MILLION

162 MILLION

137 MILLION

105 MILLION

84 MILLION

66 MILLION

65 MILLION

46 MILLION

32 MILLION

24 MILLION

answering enquiries in a mock self-deprecating mode. Perhaps. And perhaps there is something we should be more repulsed by than the sight of a Labour leader, arse tightly wedged between the foam-filled cushions, fielding questions on his private life and the state of the knowledge economy, coyly making himself available to our collective assent. Maybe. The contrast is, of course, stark—'Now, Prime Minister, if we could turn for a moment to foreign policy ...' But the meaning of this particular tableau is not to be found in the contrast ; the meaning is in the appeal, and the appeal is directly to our seated selves. Sit down, pull up a chair, settle back, have a seat. Anything we can get you? Postal vote? 'To give them light that sit in darkness and in the shadow of death.' Again, from Luke, we receive wisdom and truth.

When I was a child I spake as child, I understood as a child, I thought as a child and every night on television there were large groups of men, wearing T-shirts and baseball caps, standing up. They stood for months, years it seemed to me, and then every so often people would address them standing up, and then others would stand to support their standing until all across the country whole areas were standing up. Many have stood. Simon Stylites stood up for his God. Martin Luther King. Aneurin Bevin. Odysseus, strapped against the mast, ears blocked against the sirens. Rosa Luxemburg. Rosa Parks. 'Then on the shore/Of the wide world I stand alone.' 'Behold, I stand at the door, and knock.' 'Yea,' said he, 'that I do : that you stand out of my sun a little.'

'GO AND WALK THROUGH THE LAND, AND DESCRIBE IT.'

JOSHUA—(18:8)

Policy Initiative No. 4 : On the correct bearing for the citizenry, whether to be sitting or to be standing, *The Enthusiast* says, 'Stand Up!'

B. ANMER *(Peterborough)*

What do you stand for?

theenthusiast@theenthusiast.co.uk

THE ENTHUSIAST, PO BOX 239, BANGOR, BT20 5YB

The Enthusiast is currently seeking a...

Business Manager

YOU

. . . **WANT TO BE PART OF A UNIQUE OPPORTUNITY** to transform the world of magazine publishing.

. . . **HAVE REAL LEGITIMACY** and credibility because, in whatever sector, you have been there and delivered.

. . . **ARE A RIGOROUS PROJECT MANAGER.**

. . . **ARE ANALYTICAL** and can abstract from experience and apply the learning elsewhere.

. . . **ARE RESULTS-ORIENTATED**, can-do, flexible, creative, and most of all a deliverer.

. . . **HAVE EXPERTISE** in magazines, film, radio, television, education, local government, health, agriculture, conflict resolution, banking, accountancy, dentistry, or the criminal justice system; really, anything.

THE JOB

To enhance the competence and capacity of *The Enthusiast* to deliver our programme of encouragement and reform, particularly in the areas of literature, music, the arts, education, local government, gardening, cookery, and criminal justice.

MAIN DUTIES AND RESPONSIBILITIES—

Lead and contribute to projects across *The Enthusiast*, in particular areas promoting ways of working and changes that lead to the achievement of *The Enthusiast*'s vision of a world-class magazine.

Build relationships between *The Enthusiast* and the private and public sectors, concentrating on particular key agreed linkages, to gain real traction with readers, subscribers and stakeholders, and to gain a wide ownership and support for *The Enthusiast*'s transformation agenda.

Prepare, present and debate reports in support of *The Enthusiast*'s work to a wide variety of audiences – colleagues, wider partners, public and private sector bodies.

Identify good practice throughout the public, private and voluntary sectors both nationally and internationally and seek practical ways of instilling better practice as part of *The Enthusiast*'s publishing programme.

Contribute to the development of policy regarding the involvement of the private sector in the magazine's funding.

THE PERSON

COMMUNICATING AND INFLUENCING—

Essential: Successful track record of engaging effectively with others, building productive working relationships and partnerships which may have included a variety or some combination of communities, partner organisations, private sector providers, Government, public agencies and statutory authorities.

Demonstrable experience of analysis and producing top quality written material that can communicate complex concepts in ways that are easily understood to a wider audience.

CONTINUOUS IMPROVEMENT / DELIVERING RESULTS—

Essential: A track record of demonstrable success in change management and changing cultures across diverse organisations, in a way that has successfully turned around services or influenced departures from traditional ways of working.

CUSTOMER FOCUS—

Essential: A track record of focusing on customer needs and building these constantly into the operation and processes of the organisation. An excellent understanding of customer issues in the end-to-end delivery chain.

LEADING AND DEVELOPING OTHERS / WORKING TOGETHER—

Essential: Experience at senior level of vision-led leadership, leading and delivering substantial strategic and service improvement, ideally where change has been designed around the customer, and managers/staff have been rewarded and held to account for delivering high standards in a devolved framework.

An understanding of how to structure programmes of reputation-enhancement and influence across a wide range of stakeholders.

Demonstrable project experience as both team/project member and project manager.

Comfortable working within a loose matrix management structure; strongly self-motivated.

Willing to work initially on a commission-only basis.

Is this you?

theenthusiast@theenthusiast.co.uk
The Enthusiast, PO Box 239, BANGOR BT20 5YB

Hut

All my life I have wanted to disappear. For as long as I can remember, and I strongly suspect for longer than that–for as long, I would guess, as I have had an inkling–my deepest desire, I would even call it my ambition, has been to make a disappearance. I don't think this is strange. I think most people want to disappear. I see people trying to do it all the time. Only usually they don't pull it off, because it is a thing about disappearing–there is a right way but there are also wrong ways to go about it.

So to be clear, when I say 'All my life I have wanted to disappear' I don't mean, for instance, that I want to emulate Lord Lucan. I haven't to my knowledge, which is of course only limited–not unusually limited perhaps, but very limited all the same–committed any terrible crimes; no triple murders, no acts of treason, no tax evasions, no jumped ships; nothing, in other words, I would find it necessary to flee from, no corner of my history I am looking to evade. Which is not to imply that my record is by any stretch clean–there have been the usual riots of mutual abuse, routine bouts of psychological torture–only that when I say disappearance I don't mean flight.

Nor do I mean that I have an escape fantasy, although I do of course participate in this aspect of the nation's cultural life–whenever I watch television, for instance, or browse the Sunday papers, I get this uncanny feeling it would be nice to live in the Maldives; which I haven't ever visited nor investigated in detail, in fact if I'm honest I'd be hard pushed to locate them on the map. Still, though, there are times when I am certain I want to live there ; I consider this my contribution to the lowering of the National Debt. Nor could I say that there haven't been nights in my life when I haven't lulled myself to sleep with the thought of walking away from it all; wandering off–maybe one last check on my email–a quiet farewell to my circumstance. Only I haven't, and have no intention of doing so. All things considered I rather like my circumstances. Which is odd because as far as I can tell what these mostly consist of is putting the bins out, which I do without fail–we have a wheelie bin, and then every other Monday we have transparent bags in which we are encouraged to recycle: tins, paper, cardboard, plastic. I have always suspected they burn the bags. Here, for the record, are some of my other circumstances, which I have tried to tabulate for ease of reference. The times allocated (weekly) are an estimate only, but they bear some relation to the fabric of my life:

fig.1

	CIRCUMSTANCE	TIME SPENT ENGAGED IN CIRCUMSTANCE	DEGREE (OUT OF 10) TO WHICH I DON'T MIND IT
1	Shopping *(supermarket)*	3 hours	2
2	Shopping *(local stores)*	20 mins	6
3	Checking bank balance *(ATM)*	30 mins	5
4	Checking bank balance *(Telephone)*	1 hour	7
5	Putting bins out	15 mins (25 when recycling)	6
6	Being in the garden	2 hours 30mins	8
7	Running, jogging actually	1 1/2 hours (This an overestimate)	8
8	Completing forms	2 hours	6
9	Idling	Too difficult to say	10
10	Tidying up	7 hours	6
11	Relating	5 hours and 40 mins	8
12	Other	The Rest	Varies

There are others of course, more occasional in nature, and therefore more difficult to quantify, for instance, shaking off the dew, listening to birdsong, sex, mending unreliable appliances. And all in all, taken as a weave, as the woofing and warping of a finite life, I would have to say that I don't mind these circumstances; in fact all the efforts of television to persuade me otherwise, and the Maldives notwithstanding, I would say that I miss them.

Which means, I think, that I am not suicidal either, or at least that my ambition is not to become a suicide–there is something about the adjective I think I could live with; the noun, on the other hand, I can live without. Which is not to say that I am not sometimes downcast. In fact I would probably say that I am cast down on an almost daily basis. That rarely a day goes by–I have taken to marking them in my diary (I use that smiley face with which people sign off email)–when I don't at some point slip into the slough of despond, speculating inconsolably on the purpose of my existence. But this is routine of course, and to date I have always pulled out of it, and for the pulling out I can recommend circumstance, especially, from the above, 2, 6, and 7, and from the occasional ones I mentioned the first 3, although the fourth can be good from the point of view of distraction; I would tend, however, to avoid 1, 4 and 9. Sometimes, of course, it takes longer to pull out than others: whole weekends can go by when even 6 won't do it. Even so I've never contemplated taking a knife and a bottle of pills, and making myself comfortable in a nearby forest. Nor has it ever occurred to me to strap explosives to my back, book

a table at a local restaurant, eat a starter and the best part of a hearty main course, then blow the whole place to smithereens. These, it strikes me, are wrong ways to disappear, though in part naturally it's a question of temperament, and then of course if somebody puts a shell through your front room, probably you'll be inclined to do something extreme; and then if the somebody seems to have the whole weight of global capital behind them, and you've got a job on to find a clean glass of water, picking your way always through yesterday's debris, I guess the odds start to look stronger in favour of self-obliteration. None of this, however, is to be recommended.

For myself, when melancholy really sets in, when the woman who checks my balance seems to have taken against me, when my border arrangements start to fill me with anguish, when I find myself flicking through brochures for the Maldives, when the comfortable rhythms of my daily existence come to seem the trammels on which my fate is inexorably laid down, when I wake up howling in the face of an empty universe–I know it is time to take myself for a walk. I used to walk in cities, and by and large I enjoyed the experience, the multiple opportunities for getting lost, the poking about in unlikely retail outlets, the anonymous encounters with the world's traffic; only what I began to realise was that no matter how far I wandered, and how far in my wandering I allowed myself to digress, how drawn I might have become to a particular building or object, I always ended up beside a body of water: canals and rivers if the city was landlocked, ports and harbours if it was maritime. Once I realised this, and it was some years before I did so–I catch on quickly except where my own motives are concerned–I moved to the coast, or at any rate to the estuary; to that estuarial outpost which is to all intents and purposes the sea.

I have never been quite certain why, when the brochures start to pile up, a walk along the sea becomes the only adequate response, although I am certain that other people accumulate brochures also, because whenever I am out walking I am rarely alone. Not that we speak much, us Estuarians, not, anyway, when we are in Estuarial mood. A nod, maybe, in the direction of fellow feeling, but it is only recent arrivals that go as far as volunteering a word. As for why we do it, and obviously I can only speak for myself here, I would say that the attraction is not as one might think the tidal ebb and flow; nor is it the opportunity for reflection, because who in their right minds ever opted to reflect–on anything, let alone their own place in the world–that way self-detonating rucksacks lie. No, if there is a reason, and quite likely it is the absence of one, the appeal perhaps lies in the play of depth and surface, or just in the surface, or the way the surface alters, or the fact that the surface is capable of alteration. Whatever, there are evenings in my life when I go for a walk, breathe the air in, push the air out, participate locally in the general circulation of matter, start to speculate, maybe, on the great questions of the world: like whether the universe runs on to an infinite series, backwards and forwards, with no end ever in sight, or whether somehow it just all started up, on the whim, perhaps, of some catastrophically bored creator; and if there was a beginning, what preceded the beginning, and if there is to be an end, what comes after the end. Silence, maybe, or perhaps a barely audible whistling–the unostentatious, quietly satisfied sound of someone who made something happen.

You can never be certain of the backwards look obviously, and I guess my hindsight is no more bankable than the next person's: though my parents, it should be said, always emphasised fidelity. This I took to be the first lesson. Even so it is clear to me now, from the relative comfort of my timber-framed hut, that my ambition, though not in a general way unusual, has, nonetheless, been quite specific. So when I say disappear, I don't mean vanish–there was to be no liquidation of assets, no clothes on the beach–nor escape, nor abscond, not make my way up the ladder, not sitting on the sofa with Fern Britton; not working, not shopping, not making myself presentable–I tried that once, and it doesn't work; not applying myself, not letting myself go, not fasting, not fading, not eating myself up; not getting lost in translation, not becoming invisible, though that has its attractions, not slipping from view. No, I mean 'to disappear'; I mean to make a disappearance; I mean to appear to disappear. The hut helps. I bought it from a man who had evidently taken good care of it. He had divided the space into separate areas. There was a space for cooking and a space for sleeping. Then in the middle there was what he called the living area. The whole place was furnished elegantly, if sparsely. He had also taken the trouble to wire the place up, so I have electric lighting, a small fridge, a short-wave radio, and a two-ring stove. When I bought it, it was with a view to long summer evenings: it has a good-sized deck pointing directly on to the beach. I imagined barbecues, bottles of Chianti. Only recently, increasingly, I have found myself making much more use of the place. I invent tasks, find myself reasons to come here: stripping back the paintwork, sanding the deck. For as long as I can remember I have been trying to disappear.

Imagine the pleasure of finally making it happen.

DAVID HERD *(Whitstable)*

How's Your Garden?

theenthusiast@theenthusiast.co.uk

THE ENTHUSIAST, PO BOX 239, BANGOR, BT20 5YB

EVERYTHING IS GOING TO BE ALRIGHT

BEN COVE (*Manchester*)

– ADVICE –

...TO POACHERS
Be firm with your ferrets.
Carry rabbits by the ears.
Hold your cigarette in sheltering palm.

BOB WELLER *(Beardon)*

...ON GLUE
Common sticky tape should never be used for repairs: fresh animal or fish glue is much better.

MRS. I. CULKERTON *(Daventry)*

...ON HOME PRESERVATION
There are people who do preserve successfully. You need jam-jar seals, a cherry stoner, a poultry divider, and a packing spoon. And you need to choose your corks very carefully.

BRIAN HUGHES *(Grayrigg)*

...ON AESTHETICS
We dwell on the contemplation of the beautiful because this contemplation strengthens and reproduces itself.

IMMANUEL KANT *(Königsberg)*

Help us with anything?

– WHAT I NEED –

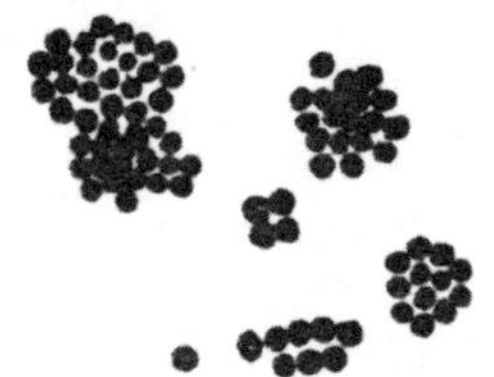

I need some sort of ointment for this itch.

LYNN PRESTON *(Manchester)*

Pox?

– CORRECTIONS AND CLARIFICATIONS –

WE are glad to be able to offer some further corrections and clarifications. Yes, we're sorry, you were right : it's a *batch* of bread ; a *bundle* of rags ; the grass isn't always greener ; no, we did not mean to suggest a lack in your book-learning ; yes, the proper name is chutney ; if you're the first on the scene, of course you mustn't panic and don't run ; no, fatalities cannot be excused by excessive feelings ; yes, really, this is it ; and the correct phrase is 'epoch-making gesture'.

Any errors?

- THINGS TO MAKE AND DO -

How to make a Mermaid

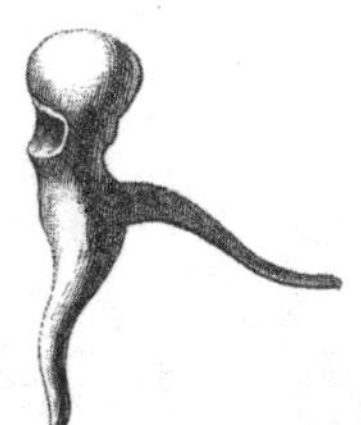

You will need: *One female orangutan*

*

One large baboon

*

One large salmon

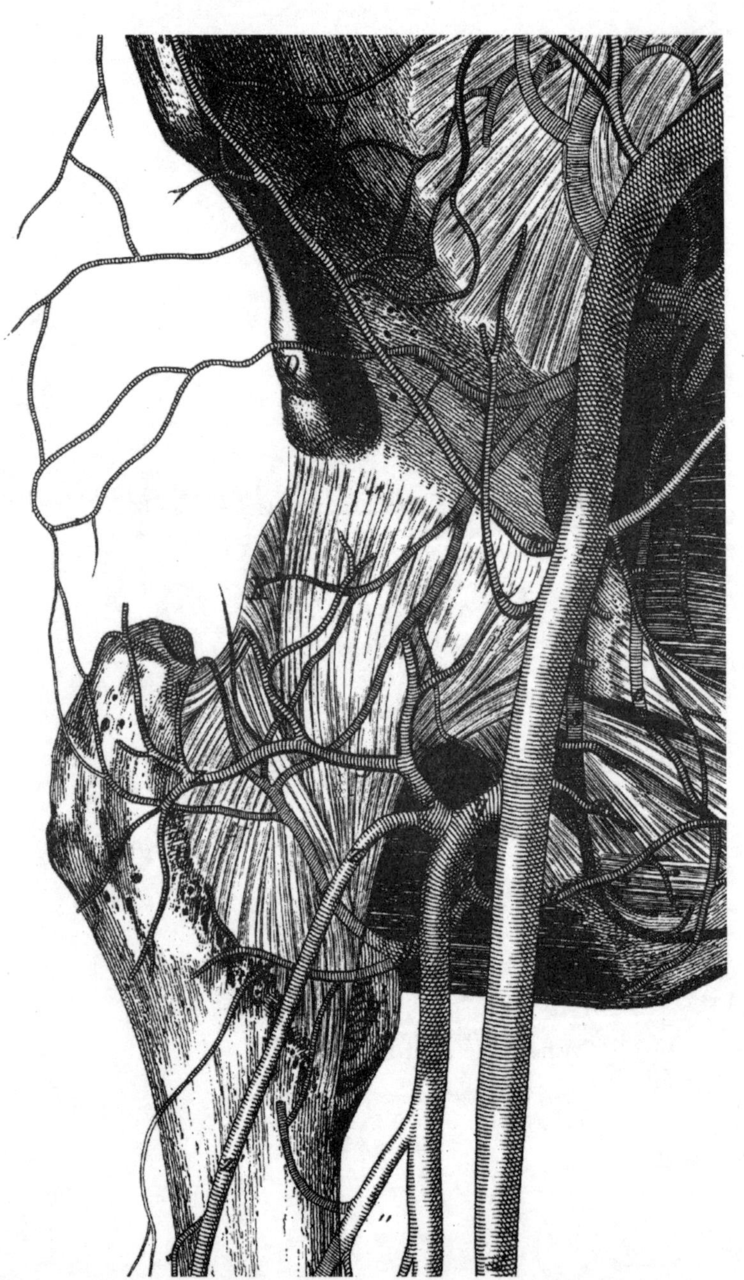

1
Take one female orang-utan, full grown. Kill.

2
Remove arms, legs, jaws, teeth, and eyes.

3
Form nose and ears from folds of skin.

4
Take one large baboon, full grown, male or female. Kill.

5
Discard torso and head. Keep jaws and teeth: insert into cranium.

6
Break or saw bones of lower arm, under the skin.

7
Insert nails into fingers: horn or quill.

8
Stuff the breasts.

9
Separate head of salmon immediately behind the gills.

10
Join.

11
(Optional) Use wooden hoop to distend body of fish from pectoral to the anal fins.

IAN SANSOM *(Bangor)*

What else could we do?

theenthusiast@theenthusiast.co.uk
THE ENTHUSIAST, PO BOX 239, BANGOR, BT20 5YB

Don't know what to listen to?

Some ideas and recommendations

1. **HENRY MAKOBI: NEW MEMORIES** *(Music and Words)*. Delightful and intimate guitar playing from Kenya.

2. **WOOB: 1194** *(Em:t Records)*. Hard to find but seminal ambient record.

3. **BERT JANSCH: BERT JANSCH** *(Castle)*. A nice bit of the old jingly jangly.

4. **VARIOUS: NU-PROGRESSIVE ERA** *(Hooj Choons)*. Progressive house *can* be wonderful and here's how.

5. **TORU TAKEMITSU: CHAMBER MUSIC** *(Naxos)*. Intoxicating pieces of music from the minimalist composer.

6. **RYUKYU UNDERGROUND: RYUKYU UNDERGROUND** *(Riverboat Records)*. Splashes of Ryukyu island folk with western beats and programming.

7. **AUTECHRE: GARBAGE** *(Warp)*. Pulsating, deep, and affecting. Perfect electronica.

8. **DUMISANI MARAIRE & EPHAT MUJURU: SHONA SPIRIT** *(Music of the World)*. Terrific thumb piano playing from two Zimbabwean masters.

9. **LOUIS ANDREASEN: QUAVAAT** *(ULO)*. Charming and sadly deceased accordion maestro from the south of Greenland.

10. **KENNY BURRELL: MIDNIGHT BLUE** *(Blue Note)*. You must have some jazz and this is near perfect guitar-led stuff.

11. **ROOTS MANUVA: BRAND NEW SECOND HAND** *(Big Dada)*. Deep English hip-hop of many superlatives!

12. **TARAF DE HAÏDOUKS: HONOURABLE BRIGANDS, MAGIC HORSES & EVIL EYE** *(Cramworld)*. Incredible Romany folk from out of Romania.

13. **VARIOUS: A ROOM FULL OF TUNEFUL** *(Melodic)*. Start your love affair with Melodic records! Disarming and dreamy; indie and trip-hop together.

14. **LOITUMA: IN THE MOONLIGHT** *(Northside)*. Gorgeously rendered folk from Finland.

15. **PANDIT SHIVKUMAR SHARMA: THE VALLEY RECALLS** *(Hemisphere)*. A Classic recording of traditional Indian pieces.

16. **DINOSAUR JUNIOR: WHERE YOU BEEN** *(Warner)*. Sadly overlooked band pioneering grunge rock and magical solos.

17. **VARIOUS: DUB COMBINATIONS** *(Kog)*. New Zealand: hotbed of the brilliant new wave of dub!

18. **MUM: FINALLY WE ARE NO ONE** *(Fatcat Records)*. Special folk-tronica and lullabies from Iceland.

19. **TELEK: TELEK** *(Origin)*. One man in Papua New Guinea fusing traditional music and song-writing brilliantly.

20. **STARS OF THE LID: THE TIRED SOUNDS OF STARS OF THE LID** *(Kranky)*. Even more silence. Lush organic music.

LEE MATTHEWS *(Orpington)*

Need music to distract you from the yawning void?

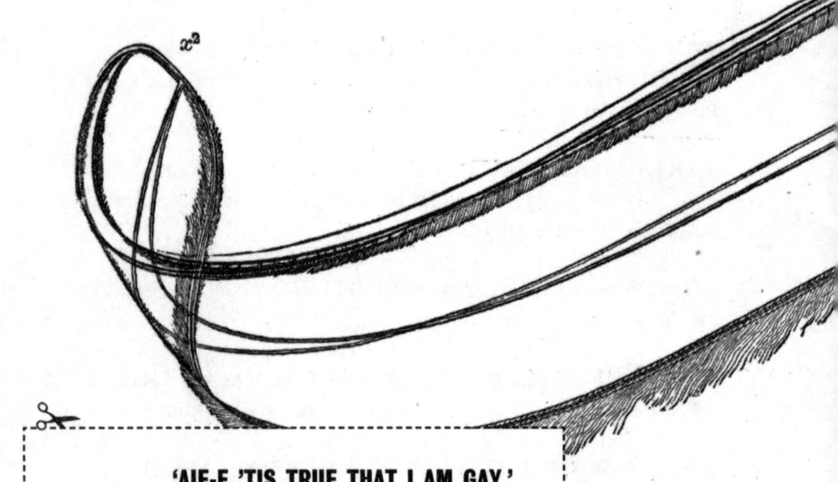

'AIE-E 'TIS TRUE THAT I AM GAY.'

EZRA POUND—(La Fraisne)

LIVES OF THE FAMOUS

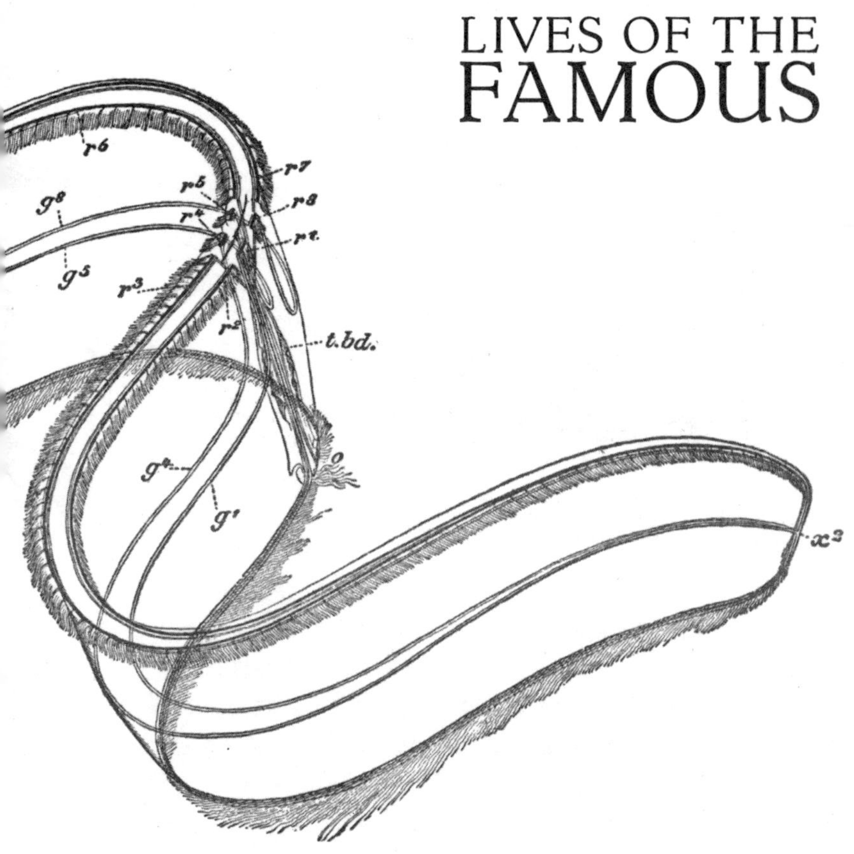

LORD CHESTERFIELD—Lord Chesterfield, in a famous letter to his son warning him against laughter, wrote, 'In my mind there is nothing so illiberal, and so ill-bred, as audible laughter . . . I am neither of a melancholy, nor a cynical disposition; and am as willing, and as apt, to be pleased as anybody; but I am sure that, since I have had the full use of my reason, nobody has ever heard me laugh.' Chesterfield had good reason to keep his laughter to himself.

According to Lord Hervey, in his *Memoirs*, Chesterfield was not merely 'a person as disagreeable as it was possible for a human figure to be without being deformed', being 'clumsily made', 'short, disproportioned, thick' and with 'a broad rough-featured ugly face', but he also had bad teeth. He was therefore wise to keep his mouth shut. The portrait of Chesterfield painted by Gainsborough in 1768 shows him thin-lipped and toothless.

MIMA CAESAR *(Manchester)*

Rictus grin?

*   WISE WORDS * *

'IT WAS A SONG THAT ASCHENBACH COULD NOT REMEMBER EVER HAVING HEARD BEFORE; A BOLD HIT IN AN UNINTELLIGIBLE DIALECT, AND HAVING A LAUGHING REFRAIN IN WHICH THE REST OF THE BAND REGULARLY AND LOUDLY JOINED. AT THIS POINT BOTH THE WORDS AND THE INSTRUMENTAL ACCOMPANIMENT STOPPED AND NOTHING REMAINED EXCEPT A BURST OF LAUGHTER.'

THOMAS MANN—(Death in Venice)

Peter! Peter!

A NOH PLAY

'The Noh plays are ancient one-act plays of Japan. The audience once dressed for them as for a religious service in elaborate ceremonial robes. The interest is in suggested action or tensions, and in the lyrics, dances and formalized gestures. The decor is symbolical. The musicians–traditionally three dancers, and a flute–appeared on stage. The actors stamped their feet at the conclusion of their speeches. The movement is photographic rather than dramatic. The audience is supposed to know all the plays by heart.'

THE PERSONS

VOICE 1—will tend, on the whole, to be grumpy
VOICE 2—is something of a flash in the pan

* The voices alternate. There *is* only one act. *

THE PLAY

SCENE—The open road. At one end of which, beneath a small mountain, a dwelling welcomes the disconsolate eye; at the other a pond, still, murky, stands in the shade of a great oak. Mountain, pond, oak, dwelling: all are painted in uprights to the side of the stage. A lay-by stands equidistant between them: the distances marked out clearly on the stage floor. Two men, voice v1 and v2 arrive, grateful, exhausted at said lay-by. They have been walking all night. The sun rises. Something heavy is on their minds.

PETER–[For some hours now v1 has been silent. He is wearing a yellow and orange cloak. He raises his arms, as if himself sun-like. His speech is to be uttered in a tonally neutral voice.]

PETER–[Nodding–v2–until now also silent–nodding in recognition; his cloak is mauve.]

[They sit; each knowing there will be much more walking. It is not clear to the audience why they have stopped. They stand up. They sit down again. Each is emphatically not comfortable.]

PETER–[In this case the stress should be distributed evenly; each syllable stretched beyond its normal extent. One might think of a hyphen, Pe-ter; there is also a discernible shift in tone: not cross exactly, quietly exasperated, towards tetchy. He stands up. Only as he stands up, as he tries to stand up, his leg becomes caught in the fold of his cloak. (Left *or* right; the actor may choose here; which ever tends best towards a graphic effect.)]

[Because what ensues is the play's single most dramatic moment. v1 after much tugging and wrestling–the audience should be thinking here of Harold Lloyd, in an early masterpiece like *Good Cop, Fat Cop*–finally manages to haul himself up. Except that in hauling–and what should be emphasised here is effort, cartoon gestures signalling frustration and sweat–he has pushed his right foot (the actor's left is acceptable) through and into the hem of his coat. So that while he *is* up, he is only partially upright; the cloak is shin-length, so as it tightens, he stoops; and he is hopping, a picture of unaccountable fury, trying to work his entangled foot loose. Except that in working he kicks, pushing his foot further into the hem, and with each time he kicks, so the hood of his cloak is pulled down, and as he kicks he hops, so now he is kicking *and* hopping; the unavoidable comparison is with a demented hen. And this –kick, hop, head lurching involuntarily; the image of a body uselessly at war with itself–goes on for minutes, to many it seems like hours; to some it seems like the rest of their life. Except that of course v1, having arrived exhausted, cannot sustain this expression of purposeless rage, so he collapses, breathless, beside his companion, his voice breaking into a barely audible wail.]

PEEEEEEEETERRRRRRRRRRR–[The wail, haunting, weirdly entrancing–the audience by this time is on the edge of its seat–drifts preternaturally across the landscape, one is reminded inescapably of Tennyson's Maud. And on it goes, barely altering in intensity–an expression, eventually of pure duration, except that as such it becomes clear the sound must necessarily be taped, only the break is seamless, so one minute the actor is sounding, the next spectacularly voiceless, mute. Gapes. The effect is of noise through silence. The mouth's silence outlined by the continuous noise, shaped, attributed definition, until to everybody present the differential is clear. Whereupon, and here the judgement is technical, although in practice the moment is always the same, the pitch drops, steeply, disarmingly; the engineered voice becomes a clarinet. And sings, briefly, the allusion is to America, to Aaron Copland after World War Two, but the phrase is muffled, becomes Lutoslowski, becomes Anton Webern, becomes Thomas Adès. Then nothing. And for a while the sound is only of breathing … until v2, elaborately, starts shaking his head …]

PETER—[… he mumbles, the tone is of resignation.]

PETER—[v1 also, now, is shaking his head.]

PETER—[Jointly, by way of announcement.]

PETER—[Sweetly, as if laying in bed.]

PETER—['Your Mammy is coming to get you.']

PETER—[Laughing.]

PETER—[Laughs.]

PETER—[Now they are laughing totally.]

PETER—[Laughing. The audience laughs.]

PETER—[Fuck it. Laughing. Totally.]

PETER—[Fuck it. Totally. Stops.]

[And as the lights go down so the lights go up again. v1 and v2 have left the stage. The audience rises, not sure what it has witnessed–how long it has been here. There is stamping feet.]

– ANNOUNCEMENTS AND ADVERTISEMENTS –

VICTIMS' VOICES

HAVE YOU been affected by our recent history of conflict, sometimes referred to as The War / The War on Terror / The Struggle / The Troubles / The Strife? *If you have, I want to hear from you.* I want to understand more about the needs of victims and survivors who have suffered during the many years of conflict and violence. *While government services and other support organisations try to respond positively to these needs it is clear to me that not all needs have been met.* I am determined to find out what more needs to be done. I want to see in place a strategy–with practical support–that gives victims and survivors of the conflict: recognition; acknowledgment; and, where appropriate, the necessary help to rebuild their lives. *To do this, it is important that I hear directly from those who have been adversely affected, so I am inviting views, in order to give me the information I need.* Your views will help me decide what improvements government can make. *I cannot promise to act on all views, nor can there be any 'quick fixes', but it is important that I know what people have to say.*

WRITE TO: Sylvia Thompson,
Room C.21,
Block A,
Government Buildings

OR EMAIL: theenthusiast@theenthusiast.co.uk

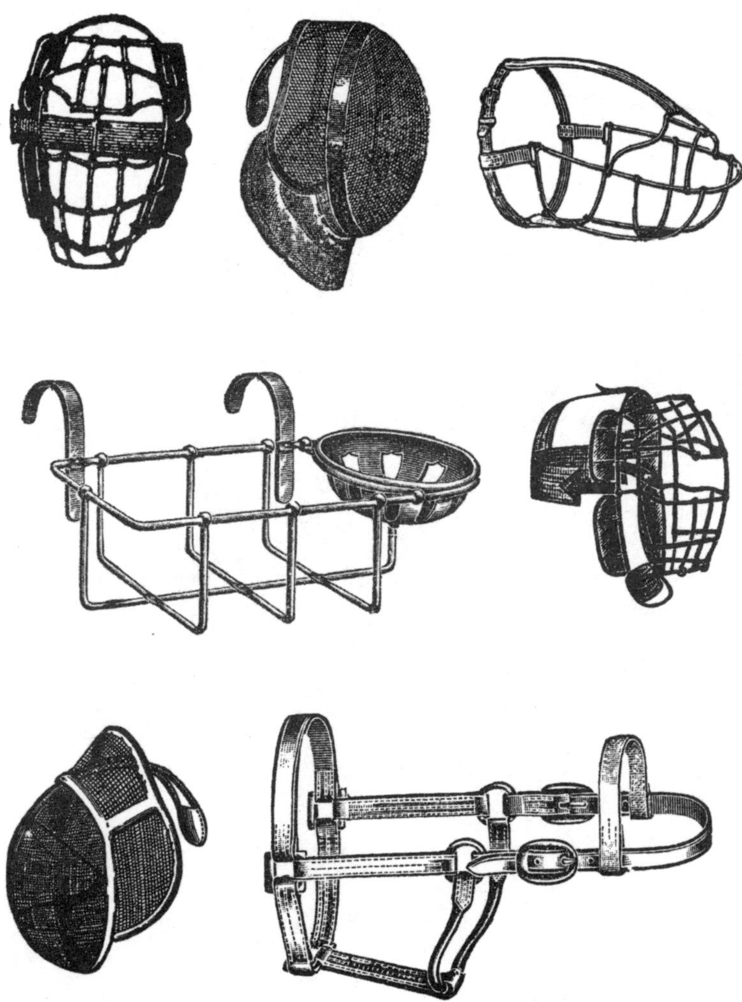

* WISE WORDS * *

'LET US NOT MINCE WORDS:
THE MARVELLOUS IS ALWAYS BEAUTIFUL,
ANYTHING MARVELLOUS IS BEAUTIFUL,
IN FACT ONLY THE MARVELLOUS IS BEAUTIFUL.'

ANDRÉ BRETON—(Manifesto of Surrealism)

Recipes

FOR AN EVENING with friends or recent acquaintances, *The Enthusiast* recommends the following menu.

Serves 6–8

PALESTINE SOUP

1 lb Jerusalem artichokes
2 onions
half stick celery
1 oz butter
1/2 pint stock
3 gills milk
1/2 gill cream
salt
lemon juice
crutons

Wash, peel and slice the artichokes. Peel and slice the onions. Wash and cut the celery into small pieces. Melt the butter in a saucepan. Fry the onions and celery for five minutes, avoiding colouring them. Add the artichokes and stir over the fire for two minutes. Pour in the stock and milk. Let it (the whole concoction) simmer gently until the artichokes are quite soft. Pass the soup through a fine sieve. Pour (the whole concoction) back into the saucepan and re-heat. Add the cream and seasoning to taste. Serve with small crutons of bread fried to a pale colour.

NB. Contrary to recent ill-informed media speculation, *The Enthusiast* would like to point out that none of its culinary advice is, in any respect, 'dubious'.

Just a drizzle?

theenthusiast@theenthusiast.co.uk

The Enthusiast, PO Box 239, BANGOR BT20 5YB

HODGE PODGE

1 carrot
2 onions
1/2 turnip
1 stick celery
1 pint stock
bunch of sweet herbs
pepper and salt
1 1/2 lbs mutton
1 pint of peas or sliced beans
1 tablespoon chopped parsley

Place the carrot, onions, turnip, celery cut up with the herbs, pepper and salt into the stock and let all simmer for 1 1/2 hours (revisiting syntax). Cut the mutton into chops or suitable pieces – here the participant will want to use his or her discretion – and add with the peas and beans into the pan. Let all simmer for a further hour. Sprinkle into the stewpan. Place the meat in the centre of a hot dish and arrange the vegetables around. Alternatively, arrange the vegetables around the meat, which should sit at the centre of a hot dish.

OLD ENGLISH CIDER CAKE

1/4 lb butter
4 oz sugar
2 eggs
8 oz flour
1 teaspoonful bicarbonate of soda
1/2 nutmeg well grated
1 teacupful cider

Beat the butter and sugar to a cream. Add the eggs, well beaten, and four ounces of flour, well sifted, along with the bicarbonate of soda and the nutmeg. Pour over all the cider beaten to a froth (taking care to revisit syntax). Mix thoroughly. Stir in the other, which is to say the remaining, four ounces of flour. Mix thoroughly. Bake in a shallow, well-greased tin, in a moderate oven for 45 minutes. This cake, when properly made, is delicious with a distinctive flavour.

Mix thoroughly.

CAROL COOPER *(Stafford)* **Well beaten?**

THE MOUSE OF THOUGHT—

Remember: there are important-sounding ways of saying simple things. There are simple-sounding ways of saying important things. Like: food is never eaten as hot as it is when cooked; hats limp in the hand take a new form on the head; it is our inner ear that makes us human; nobody is born with perfect eyebrows; paper is never plain white; this is not a bona fide hotel; this road is not a motorway; this is not what was supposed to happen.

– CORRECTIONS AND CLARIFICATIONS –

WE are glad to be able to offer further corrections and clarifications :

You can't give birth to a baby boy. Or a baby girl. It's tautologous.
COLIN FOWLES *(Birkenhead)*

Bishops are consecrated. Priests are ordained.
BARBARA DAVIES *(Swindon)*

A Bearskin is tall and furry. A Busby is flat and furry.
MICHAEL ADKINS *(Worksop)*

You centre on. You do not centre round.
TONI ARMSTRONG *(Gravesend)*

To anticipate is to forestall. To expect is to regard as likely.
JOAN ROSE *(Staines)*

Nothing better to do with your time?

---

theenthusiast@theenthusiast.co.uk THE ENTHUSIAST, PO BOX 239, BANGOR, BT20 5YB

– ADVICE –

How to fold jumpers correctly. Lay your jumper face down; fold one side in a third of the way towards the back, as if the arms are embracing; fold the sleeve down from the shoulder; repeat for other sleeve; fold the jumper crosswise at the waist.

JULIET WHITE *(Manchester)*

We all make mistakes. James Joyce wrote plays. George Bernard Shaw thought he was a novelist. Leonard Cohen published poems. Muhammad Ali did a cover version of Ben E. King's 'Stand By Me'. Blunders do not count as sins.

DR. T. HAMMOND *(Warwick)*

How to go to sleep. Personally I find counting sheep doesn't work, but let me tell you what does: imagine yourself crawling under a large upturned flower-pot, which contains inside it a smaller upturned flower-pot, and so on; or imagine yourself on a record, an LP, rotating round and round and round; or imagine monkeys riding bicycles anticlockwise round the ceiling.

MR. KNIGHT *(Southend)*

At the risk of being a bore I would like to point out once again a direction in which we want to progress. Provided we don't aim too high or go too fast or too damn seriously, there is one job which we CAN do through our boys. It is the great little service of 'happifying' ... If a boy only makes himself wear a cheery countenance in the street it is something.

ROBERT BADEN-POWELL (The Scouter, *1929*)

If you have no more tears left to weep, don't weep. Laugh.

MR. A. BROWN *(Glasgow)*

Desperate to share life's little lessons?

– WHAT I NEED –

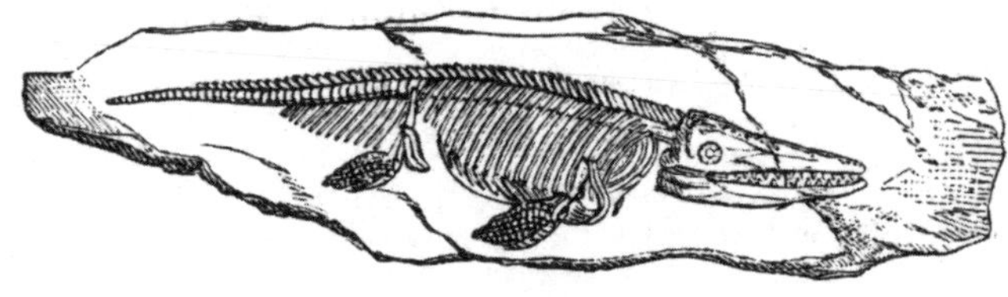

I need to learn to stop giving.
I've been giving for years.

D. ARMSTRONG *(Co. Meath)*

Me, me, me?

– THINGS TO MAKE AND DO –

How to get to: WHITSTABLE

1

Take the M2 out of London. Follow the M2 until it becomes the A2, and until the A2 splits and heads right to Canterbury. Don't go to Canterbury. Where the road splits take the A299 instead until you see the sign for Whitstable. This is you. Brake firmly and smoothly. Follow the slip road to the top of the hill. Turn left at the roundabout, averting your eyes from the Beefeater. Drop down the hill towards the sea.

(If, as you reach the top of the slip-road you find traffic stacking all the way up the hill, don't turn left at the roundabout but carry straight on until you get to Tesco, at which roundabout turn left dropping down Milstrood Road, which will take you through a number of housing estates—not at all the reason you came to Whitstable. Avert your eyes. You will eventually reach the sea.)

(A further word of advice, if Milstrood Road is stacking up also, if, say, this is a sunny Saturday in August, continue on past Tesco until you get to Ham Shades Lane. If Ham Shades Lane is backing up, go and have a cup of tea at Sainsbury's. Whatever you do, don't be tempted to press on to Margate.)

2

Take the train from London Victoria, making sure to sit in one of the front four coaches. The rear four go to Canterbury. Don't go to Canterbury.

3

Go to Soho. Drink all night at the Coach and Horses, exchanging anecdotes and vodka cocktails with your attractive friends. Go to Bar Italia. Sober up. Hail a taxi. Hail another taxi. Sleep off the vodka on a bench opposite the Houses of Parliament. Make your way up Victoria Street at the first sign of light. Take a train from Victoria, making sure to sit in one of the first four coaches. Check your messages. Text a friend.

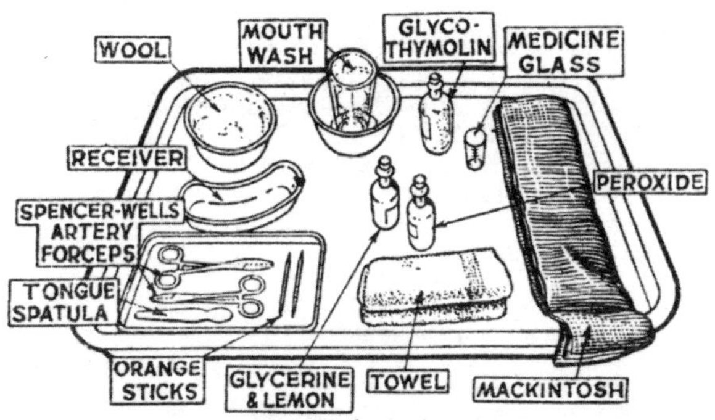

4

Ask Tracey Emin.

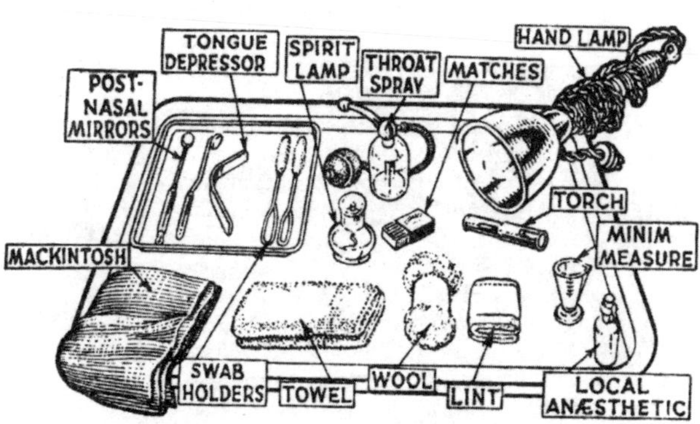

5

Ask Janet Street-Porter.

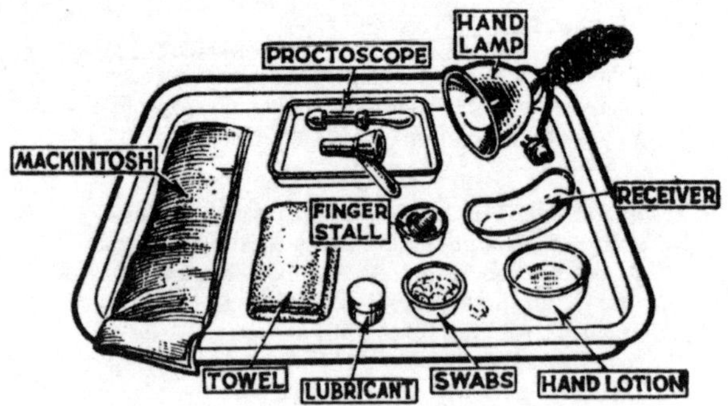

6

Follow John Lesley and Abi Titmuss.

7

Turn left at the bottom of Bleeker Street. Take the subway from Houston and Broadway. Fly out of JFK. Touch down at London Gatwick. Hail a cab. Hail another cab. Text a friend in Soho. Tell the cab driver to take the M3 and then the M25; M26, A249, M2, A299. Call Sainsbury's to book your table. Book. Text a friend. Your friend will be in Whitstable. He'll talk you down.

8

Write to a property programme.

9

Write to a property development programme.

10

Write to a television executive proposing a programme on property.

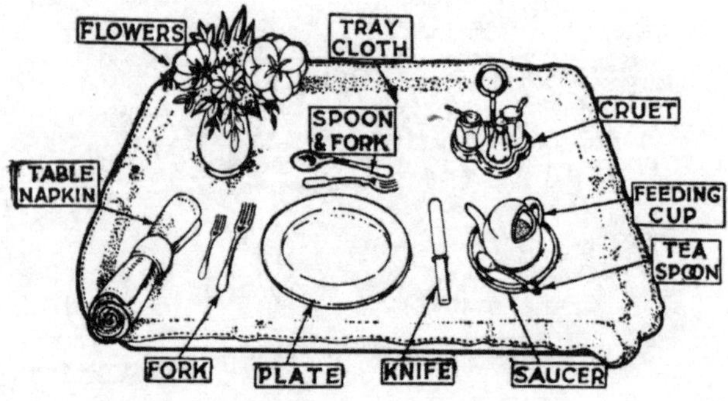

11

Ask Suggs.

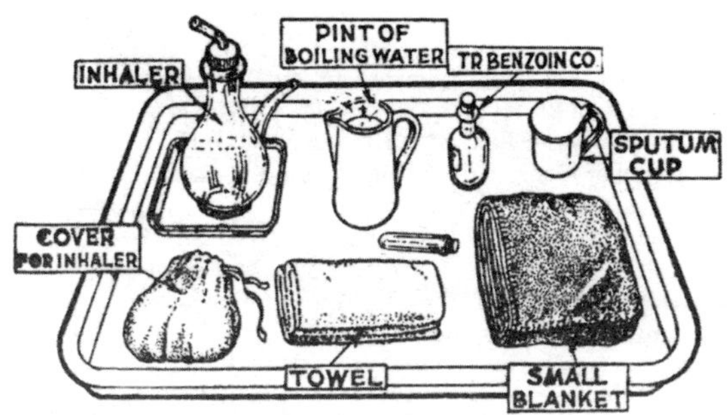

12
Ask Germaine Greer.

13
Ask anybody in Stoke Newington.

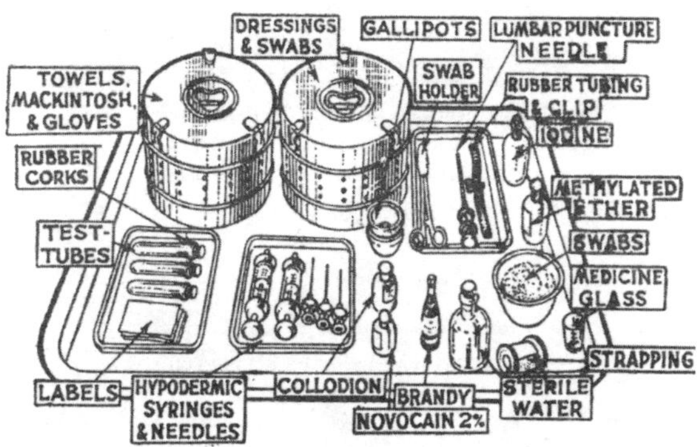

14
Ask Billy Childish.

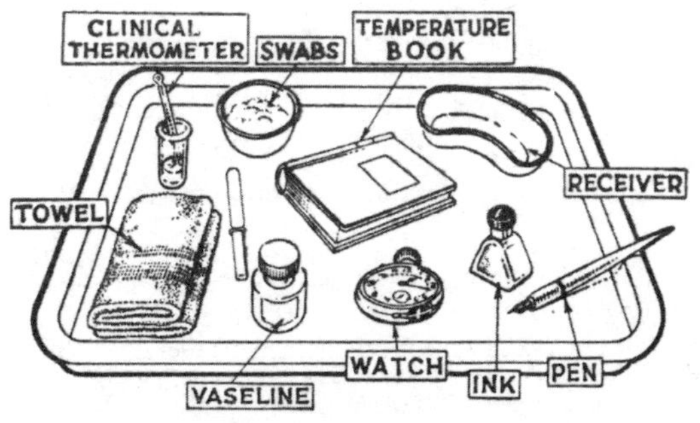

15
Don't ask Stan Collymore.

16

Leave the porter's lodge at Christchurch, Oxford, hitching a lift from the town centre to the M40. Hitch another lift with a lorry driver bound for Istanbul via Dover. Wave him farewell where the A2 splits with the A299. Hitch another lift, this time with two young men in a soft-top BMW. Tell them to turn right down Milstrood Road. Text a friend. Tell her you haven't had this much fun in years. Ask if she can cover for you at work.

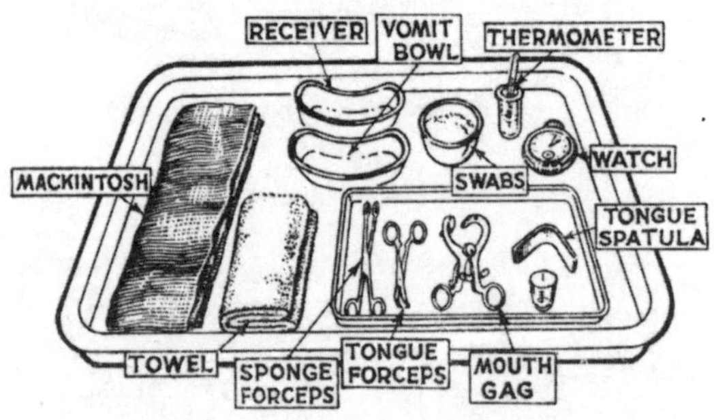

17

Ask Peter Ackroyd.

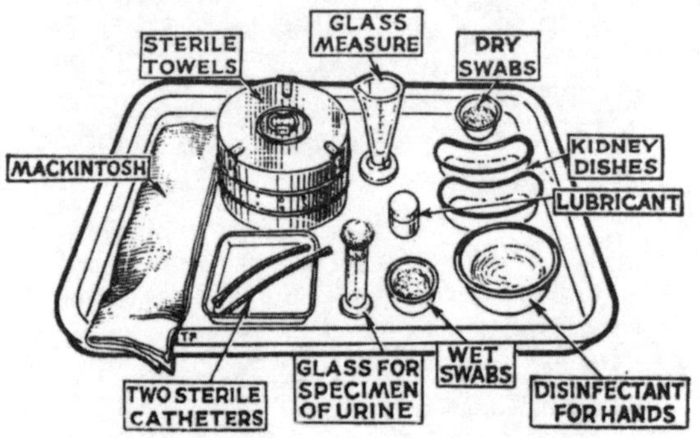

18

Ask Rowan Williams (the Archbishop of Canterbury).

19

Catch the Eurostar at Avignon, after a bar meal in Rousillon. Pick up a couple of bottles of Chablis for the journey home. Get out at Ashford International. Take the A251 to the M2. At Faversham take the coast road through the shacks of Seasalter. Follow the road round until you hit the traffic. This is Whitstable. Welcome home.

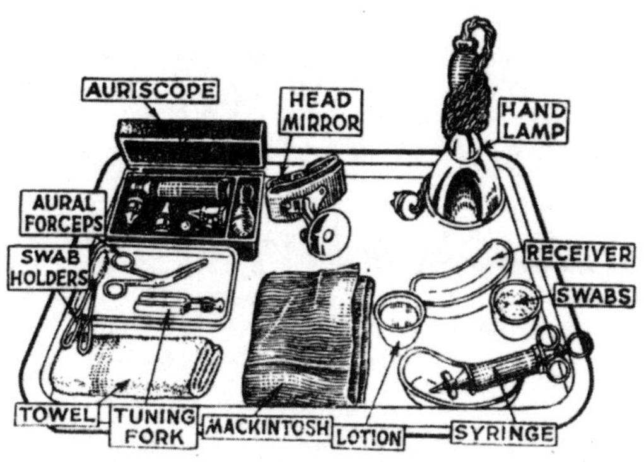

20

Ask David Dimbleby.

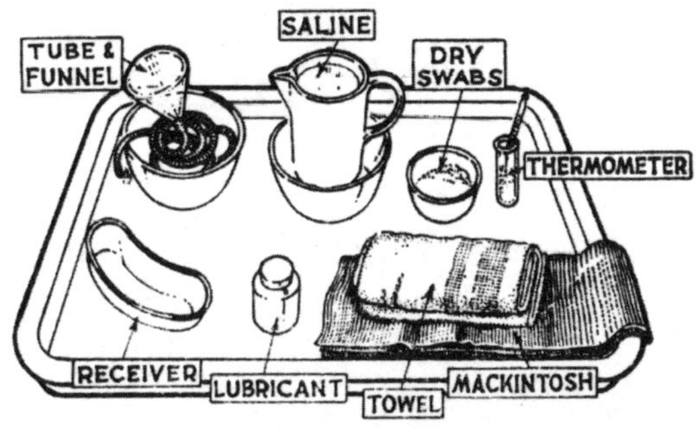

21

Ask Sarah Waters.

22

Text a friend travelling on a bus from Essaoiura to Marrakech.

23

Write to the *LRB*.

24

Download a ring-tone.

25

Check your messages.

26

Send a text.

CHET TOMPKINSON *(Whitstable)*

Absolutely no idea where you're going?

– THE ESSENTIAL PHRASE BOOK –

Elle est pesante, parce qu'elle est toute pleine de livres.

It is heavy, because it is full of books.

Er ist schwer, weil er ganz voll Bücher ist.

Pesa, perchì è pieno di libri.

JAMES CONRAD *(Newport)*

TLS?

LIVES OF THE FAMOUS

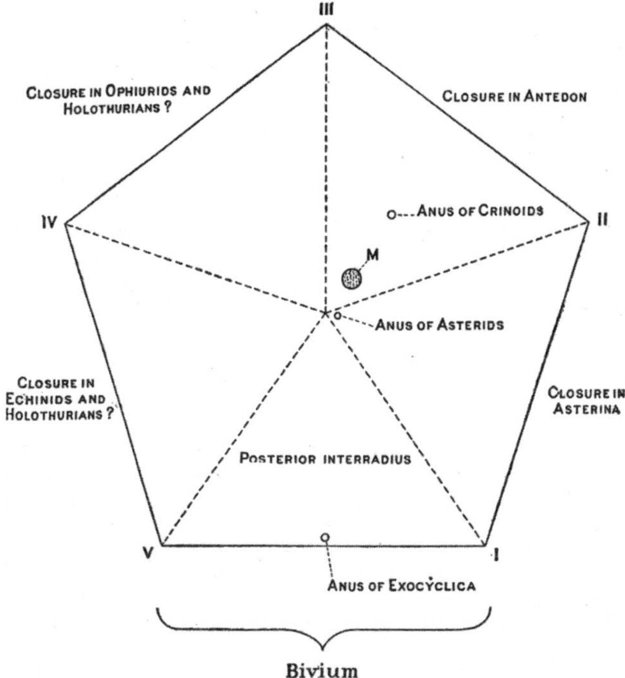

SOLOMON ECCLES—During the great plague of 1665 Solomon Eccles strode stark naked through Smithfield Fair with a dish of fire upon his head to bring home to suffering London God's judgement upon it. Given the circumstances—the plague and all—the effort hardly seemed necessary, or any more effective than his surprising wish one Sunday morning in Galway, where he demonstrated unclothed against a Catholic mass, all the while balancing a pan of fire and brimstone on his head.

Eccles exhibited other eccentricities in the Lord's service, such as commandeering the pulpit and communion table of a local London church, where he set up shop as a shoemaker in a fit of contempt for Anglican forms. A call for this kind of demonstration clearly struck Robert Barclay, the Quaker apologist, in 1672, when he traipsed through the streets of Aberdeen stark naked warning people there to repent their evil ways.

CHARLES ELLIS *(Roehampton)*

Something to shout about?

theenthusiast@theenthusiast.co.uk THE ENTHUSIAST, PO BOX 239, BANGOR, BT20 5YB

Winter

WINTER COMES AND GOES. Here at the pond, as the ice creaks against the shore, and the wind whistles in from the mid-Atlantic, and as the military personnel helicopters sketch fault lines across the horizon, we are settling down for a long, cold one. It was a beautiful autumn, all pumpkin and golden, like somebody had taken a spray can and graffitied 'wistfulness' across the trees. We picked conkers and chased squirrels, and when the air was so thick you could carve your name in it, we built a bonfire and burnt effigies of fundamentalists past. Some of the children had special fun watching the animals build their nests, though it was sad as the birds queued up along the pylons. Always this time of year brings a certain sadness – as the birds look southwards – for the summer we'd anticipated and might have had. Wasn't it this year we were going to dig a hole in the sand and cook sausages on the beach? Still there's always next year, and anyway now there's the winter to look forward to, and all that it brings to the table, all the gifts and the austerities, the quizzes and questionnaires, the parlour games and the home-made schnapps, the news of warmer, more eventful climes, and the long evenings at home with adaptations of Victorian novels, and the nights all toasty and snuggled up in bed, and the trees finally shedding all their leaves standing stark against the snow, and the robin, pecking for crumbs against the conservatory door. And to help you through it, a brand new issue of *The Enthusiast*, the spine only just now broken, the pages fresh and clean against the back of your hand, carrying all the usual fare: good humour, wisdom and throat-clearing; best wishes for your festivities, warnings of moral panic. We would, ourselves, caution against stockpiling, but then again, you can never have too many tunes on your iPod, and the winter is a good time for building up your ring-tones. Here at *The Enthusiast* we've taken to baking our own bread. In December, remember – prepare your ground.

Cold? Still cold? Colder?

- THE NATURAL WORLD -

The Consciousness of Dogs

IN POWELL AND PRESSBURGER'S wartime drama *A Matter of Life and Death*, airman Peter Carter wakes up on a deserted sunlit beach, after his Lancaster bomber has crashed. *He assumes that he is dead, and sure enough the surroundings certainly look like Heaven. Suddenly, he sees something coming towards him. 'A dog!' he murmurs, happily. 'I always hoped there'd be dogs.'*

Frances Power Cobbe (1822–1904) also believed that man's best friend would share the afterlife with us ; moreover her faith in the power of the canine mind was unshakeable. An Irish religious writer and antivivisectionist, Cobbe was an amiable and open-hearted woman, though one who could work powerfully where her sense of rectitude was engaged. Her writing on dogs verges on the obsessive ; her work remains an intriguing instance of the natural historian as amateur enthusiast, making her own last-ditch stand against the materialism of more conventionally trained scientists. The following excerpt from her essay on 'The Consciousness of Dogs' reveals both her commitment and her tenacious eccentricity.

* * *

Whether we ought to consider the marvellous faculty possessed by dogs, cats, and many other animals, of finding their way for long distances by unknown roads, as an exhibition of olfactory perception, or rather as evidence of the possession of a specific sense different from any which we have yet recognised, is a question of great interest to which it would be impossible here to do justice. In all collections of anecdotes of dogs, instances of the display of this faculty are put forward as evidences of the sagacity of the animal : but it is certain that no sagacity, in the ordinary meaning of the term, without the aid of a sense different from any known to us, would enable the creature to perform some of the feats so recorded. As cases guaranteed by living witnesses are more satisfactory than those of older date, we shall here cite two such illustrations. The Dowager Lady Stanley of Alderley, some years ago, took her Skye-terrier with her in a close barouche from Grosvenor Crescent to London Bridge. At London Bridge Lady Stanley embarked in a steamer for Gravesend, where she left Smeroch with her children, and returned to town. Next day the governess wrote to say the dog had escaped from her charge at Gravesend ; and the same night the animal appeared in Grosvenor Square, alone, footsore, and covered with mud. An equally remarkable case was that of a hound, which was sent by Mr Cobbe, from Newbridge, near Swords, County Dublin, to Moynalty, County Meath, and thence, long afterwards, was conveyed to Dublin. The hound broke loose in Dublin, and the same morning made his way back to his old kennel at Newbridge ; thus completing the third side of a triangle by a road he had never travelled in his life. Mr George Jesse gives a series of similar stories : a butcher's dog, slipping his chain and running home 120 miles, which he had been taken by railway ; an officer's dog returning 180 miles, also originally traversed by rail, etc. Strangest of all is the account given by Sir John Harington, in a letter to Prince Henry, dated 1608, of his dog Bungey, who, he affirms, often carried letters for him from his house in Bath (Somersetshire) to the Court at Greenwich ...

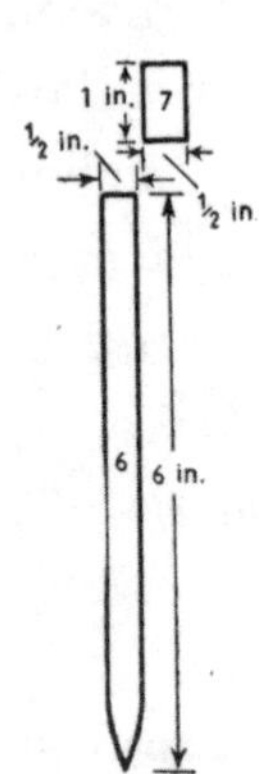

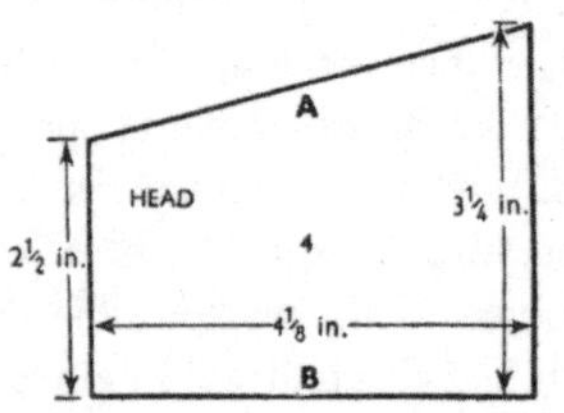

In the opinion of the writer, the theory which best explains the ascertained facts is, that the creatures in question have a certain sense of the magnetic currents, sufficient to afford them a sort of internal mariner's compass, marking the direction in which they travel. We know that the magnetic currents affect the needle, and the hypothesis that they may also affect living frames, with special organisations, seems no way incredible ; while the fact that a dog, who can find his way for a hundred miles in the open country, may lose it in five hundred yards in a town, seems to point to the multitude of streets turning at right angles as the cause of confusion to a sense which simply indicates a straight direction.[1]

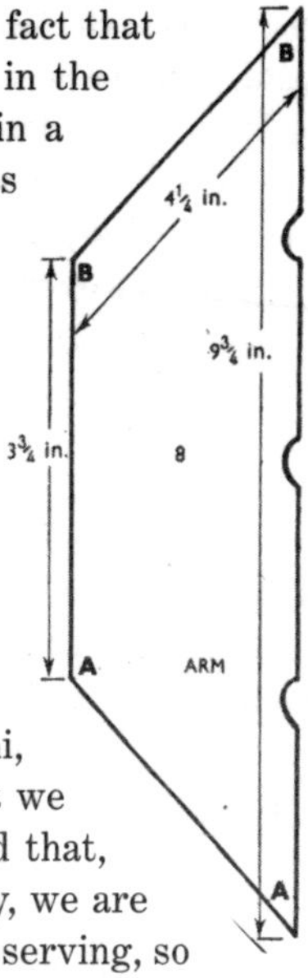

To realise then, the physical conditions of a dog, we must imagine ourselves inhabiting a diminutive and prostrate form, without hands, without speech, and destined to die of old age as a boy enters his teens ; also, as having for our special endowments a remarkable power of finding our way, and a preternaturally acute nose, accompanied by an unconquerable propensity for Ubomi, and all Ubominable things. It may be added that we should conceive our bodies covered with hair ; and that, beside the possession of great swiftness and agility, we are gifted with a peculiar caudal appendage [i.e. a tail], serving, so effectually, as a 'vehicle for the emotions', that instead of availing, like language, 'to conceal our thoughts', it should constantly and involuntarily betray our joy, sorrow, alarm, or rage ...

B
$4\frac{1}{4}$ in.
B
$9\frac{3}{4}$ in.
$3\frac{3}{4}$ in.
8
A
ARM
A

Passing beyond the physical conditions of the dog and their immediate results, we now proceed a step further towards constructing an idea of his Consciousness, by studying his Emotions, and comparing them with our own. A little reflection shows that a dog approaches a man more nearly in the matter of feeling than either of physical or mental characteristics. It is a startling fact, well brought out by Jesse in a synopsis of the dog's attributes that there are very few human passions which a dog does not share.

[1] We are indebted to Francis Galton, Esq., F.R.S., for two interesting facts corroborative of the above hypothesis. 'Reindeer kids,' says Dr Ray, 'when very young indeed, having been deprived of their mothers and left quite alone, will, in spring, always turn towards the north, however much you may try to drive them the other way.' 'Buffaloes,' (as stated by James Mackay a noted Hudson's Bay Company's guide), 'whenever they are alarmed, always run southward. This habit is so constant and so well known that, in making buffalo pounds, the entrance must always face the north, for, if it is not so placed, it is impossible to drive the animals into them.'

A dog feels *anger* precisely as we do, and after provocation is sometimes vindictive and sometimes placable, according to his individual character. He is susceptible to *hatred* of the bitterest kind. He is so excruciatingly *jealous*, that his life becomes a burden in the presence of a favoured rival ... *Gratitude* may be almost said to be a dog's leading principle, supplying first the spring of allegiance to his master, and ever after reconciling him with true magnanimity to take evil from the hand from which he has accepted good. *Regret* and *grief* he feels so deeply that they often break his heart. *Fear* is a passion which dogs exhibit with singular variation, some breeds and individuals being very timorous, and others perfect models of *courage* ; the latter characteristic, and *fortitude* seeming to be more characteristically canine. A greyhound has been known, after breaking his thigh, to run on till the course was concluded ; and in the excellent new volume 'On the Dog', by Idstone, is a frightful story of a foxhound whom its ferocious master flogged so savagely for 'babbling', as to cut out its eye with his whip. The animal continued to hunt with the pack to the end of the chase, whereupon the human brute, a certain Colonel Thornton, 'took out his scissors and severed the skin by which the dog's eye had hung pendent during the entire run' ...

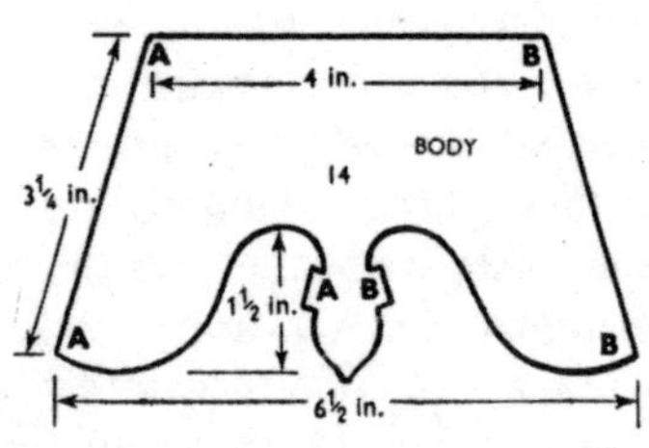

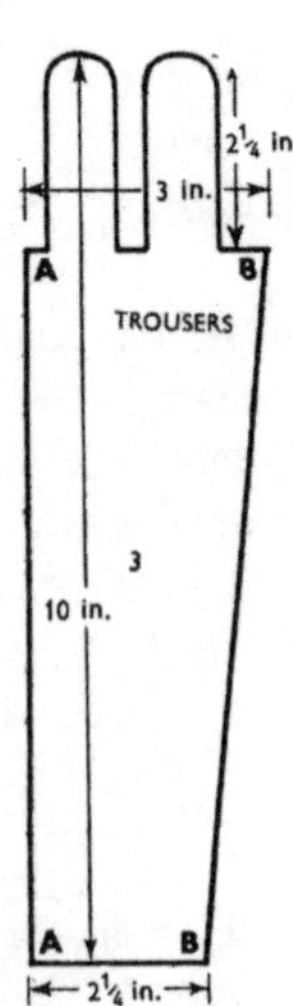

There remains now to be considered only certain higher feelings—the sympathetic, the religious, and the moral—whose possession by dogs are all commonly denied. It has been asserted over and over again, that one of the chief distinctions between man and the races below him lies in his Sympathy ... Nevertheless, it appears that the higher animals occasionally exhibit pain at the sight of the pain of others ... As to their power of sympathising with man, it is a matter concerning which no one possessed of an attached dog ever entertained a doubt ... In his description of the death of Mary Queen of Scots, Mr Froude tells us how her little dog was found to have followed her to the scaffold, hidden under her flowing robes, and that when her head had fallen, the poor creature, in the agony of its grief, lay down precisely in the severed place of the neck. Is it imaginable how the sympathy of a dumb mourner could be more forcibly expressed?

... We have seen how a dog Feels ; we must endeavour to form an idea how he Thinks ... In the first place, the mechanism of a dog's mind obviously includes several of the same wheels and pulleys as our own. He has *Memory* of persons, places, and events, extending backwards to his early youth, and it is stirred like ours, according to the same law of *association of ideas*. When his master has deserted him, and in his despair the dog takes some cast-off garment, and lies on it for days together, growling at everyone who tries to lure him away, what can we suppose he is doing? Obviously he is using the old coat or shoe to bring him nearer to his lost friend ; just as many of us have treasured a flower or a lock of hair ; or as a hagiolater kneels beside the relics of his saint ... By his dreams it is manifest that he either exactly reproduces by involuntary cerebration the precise events impressed on his memory, or, as is much more probable, that his brain, like ours, weaves them into fresh combinations. In the latter case, and supposing the dog to have a real dream of an imaginary chase after a hare, or battle with a cat, it almost necessarily follows that he can exercise the same faculty of pure Imagination awake, and that when he lies blinking in the sun or on the rug, he follows out, in his own little way, a reverie much like our own, combining what has been and what might be in a visionary scene, of which hope or fear acts as the scene-

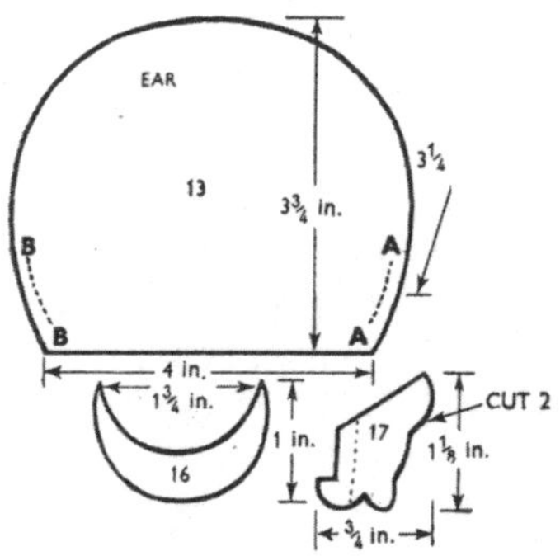

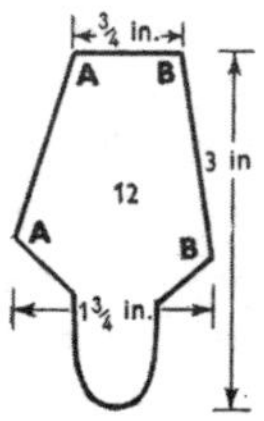

shifter. *Judgement*, or an intelligent decision between probabilities, is unquestionably one of the faculties of a dog. A clever dog is one of the best discriminators of character in the world. He distinguishes at a glance a tramp or swell-mobsman from a gentleman, even in the most soiled attire. He also has a keen sense of the relative importance of persons, and never fails to know who is the master of the house ...

Strangest and most suggestive of all the anecdotes recorded of dogs are the numerous histories of their drowning themselves, under conditions which almost compel us to class the act as voluntary and conscious suicide. Not long ago many newspapers copied a mournful story of a poor dog who was cruelly discarded in his old age by his master, and after ineffectual efforts to find shelter in another house, was seen deliberately to stand gazing at the rushing waters of the Loire, then painfully lift himself on his crippled limbs and leap into the stream. The spectator held out a stick to save him, but the beast gave him a look of despair, turned away his head, and floated down without an effort to save himself ...

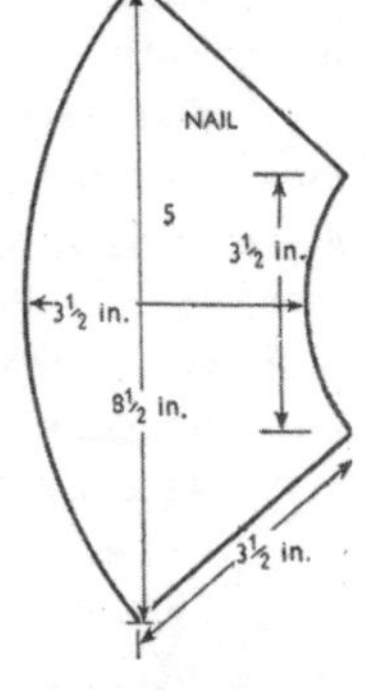

It is incumbent on us to recognise that, *so far as it goes*, the Thought of a dog is the same sort of phenomenon as the Thought of a man, carried on, doubtless, with similar modifications of cerebral matter, and being to the creature who thinks, to all intents and purposes the same action.

To comprehend what it would be to think under the conditions which limit the thoughts of a dog, we have need, in the first place, to endeavour clearly to realise what it would be to think without Language—not merely as a dumb individual in a speaking race, but as a dumb creature in a dumb race, not even possessed of hands wherewith to make an alphabet of signs ... All thought which rises above mere reverie, is a more or less defined *thinking in words* ; and the more serious and weighty are our lucubrations, and the more abstruse their theme, the more we need definite language to carry them on ... To conceive, then, the limitations of a dog's intellect, we must begin by supposing ourselves always thinking—without aid from language ; remembering—without any verbal mnemonics ; observing—without power to give a name to the thing observed ; and reasoning—without the stepping-stones of any formula, which, when once accepted, might serve as bases to the next operations.

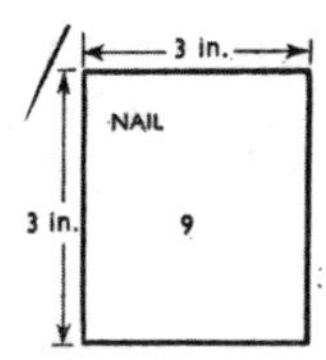

It would carry this enquiry into regions of very abstruse speculation to argue the question which here arises, 'Is the lack of language and of abstract ideas so closely involved, that the dumbness of the dog implies his want of such ideas?' We can only remark, in passing, that as a creature without words could seemingly make little or no use of such ideas, and as it is gratuitous to suppose that any creature possesses faculties both occult and superfluous, we may fairly assume that the dog possesses neither one nor the other.

Lastly, we reach the concluding problem of the dog's Consciousness. Human thought is not only occupied with its *objects*, but also carries with it more or less self-consciousness of its subject. It turns outward to the world, and also inward. Endless profound things have been written about this self-conscious 'Ich', which we carry with us in every soaring and diving of imagination and reason—this 'Ego' whose antagonism to the 'non-ego' is said to be the first perception of the awakening mind. But, whatever be its mysterious significance, are we bound to limit it to the mind of man, and to hold that the dog's mind never turns inwards—that he never thinks that marvellous thought, *I am*.

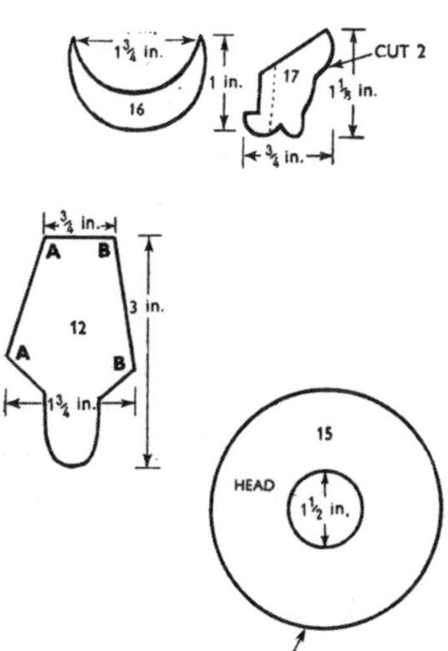

It has been long ago assumed that so it is; that the animal never gathers up Memory and Consciousness into one personality; never studies himself or compares himself with other beings, or thinks, 'I am a dog.' Such self-consciousness, the sense of moral responsibility, and the power of forming abstract ideas, are, in truth, it would appear, three phases of the same thing—three things which must exist together or not at all. If the evidence that dogs have no moral responsibility and no abstract ideas be sufficient, the further fact of their having no self-consciousness may be taken for granted ; even if the absolute simplicity of their demeanour did not bear with it an assurance, beyond need of argument, that none of the doubtings of self-introspection have ever disturbed the pellucid simplicity of their emotions and thoughts.

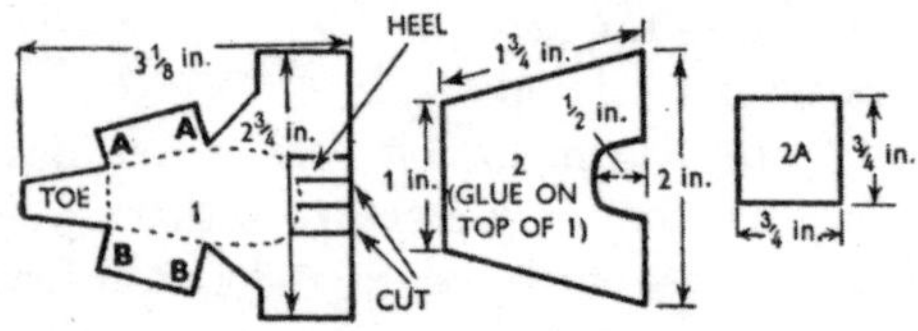

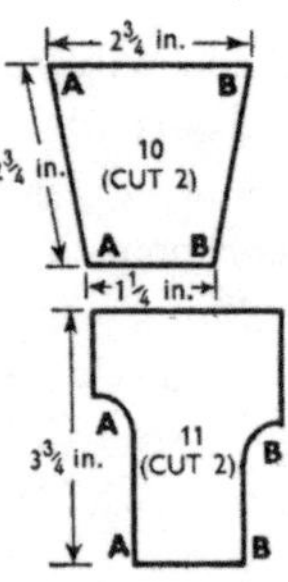

How, then, does a dog actually think, if he never carries self-consciousness along with him? Let us remember the hours when that 'Old Man of the Sea' has sat lightest on our own shoulders ; when, acting at the bidding of some strong feeling, or engrossed in some deep interest, we forgot almost entirely to reflect in our usual wearisome way that 'I' am doing this, that, or the other. Let us study the mental condition of the more light-hearted races of men, of children, and of savages. By a little further development of such experiences we shall find ourselves not far off from the point of the dog's state of mind. Merely to suppose ourselves always engrossed in what we are doing—as we are, for example, when we are reading or writing eagerly, watching a man in danger, or entering some sublime scene—and the feat is achieved. As we feel then, so the dog, in his own little sphere of interests, must feel always.

From Frances Power Cobbe, *False Beasts and True. Essays on Natural (and Unnatural) History* (London : Ward, Lock and Tyler, 1876).

MICHAEL NEWTON *(Berlin)*

Dog person? Cat person?

– RELIGION –

The Size of Heaven

469,793,088,000,000,000,000,000 cubic feet

Revelation 31:16

BERNARD HILL *(Hull)*

40 Acres and a Mule?

theenthusiast@theenthusiast.co.uk
THE ENTHUSIAST, PO BOX 239, BANGOR, BT20 5YB

THE MOUSE OF THOUGHT—

You can try all you like to hang on to your broad good humour, and your bluff good sense, and your high moral aim, and your fine tone, but sometimes people are so bad, and things get so tough, and the world seems so topsy-turvy and so unfair that all of your efforts to remain sane count for nothing. At this time of year, if you find yourself in distress, or feeling low-down and disgusted, if you find yourself having lost sight of the common good and given up hope in the human race as an evolved species, if you find yourself without, or unable to establish even the most basic of daily routines – washing, shaving, listening to Robin Lustig on *The World Tonight* – if you have given up hope, may we suggest you ask yourself this simple question: What Would Ewan McGregor Do?

LIVES OF THE FAMOUS

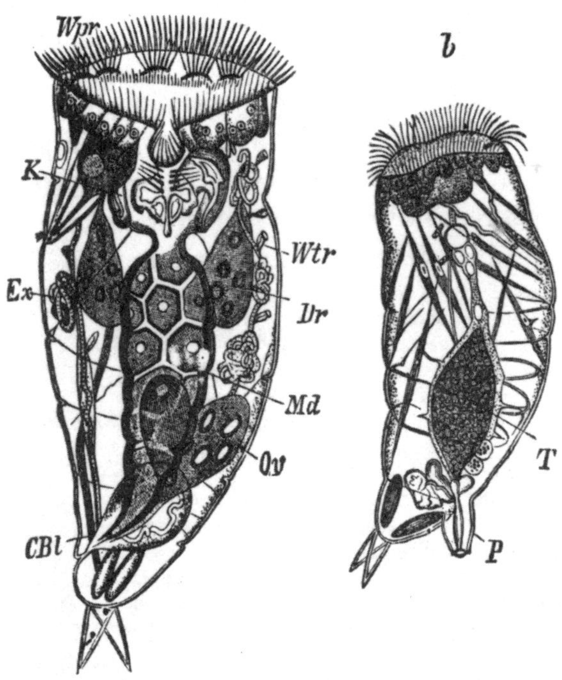

MORECAMBE AND WISE—In November 1940 the young Eric Morecambe and Ernie Wise arrived in Coventry. They were both working on Jack Hylton's touring variety show *Youth Takes a Bow* and they were supposed to be staying in the same digs in Coventry. The building, however, had been destroyed by bombing and the two had to commute daily on the train from Birmingham to Coventry with Sadie, Eric's mother.

The two boys liked to joke together on the long journey and Eric's mother Sadie suggested they work out a routine. So they did.

LESLEY DOWLING *(Hatch End)*

Chance?

- TRAVEL -

How to Avoid Ruin

Let's say you're in a boat, neither so small that you could pull it along yourself in shallow water nor so large that it requires a crew of specialists. Let's say you have to go up an unknown creek to reach your haven. Let's say you have propulsion and a device that tells you the depth of water beneath the keel. The creek like all creeks is shallow at the edges (the banks you can see) and with a deeper channel that rarely runs central. If you stray from the channel your craft will founder.

Let's say you begin on a central course but suddenly the water shallows. You do not know whether to turn left or right to find deeper water. You panic.

But there is a trick to going up a creek, and it's a beautiful trick. Avoid the centre and its unreliable reassurance of deeper water. Steer for the bank, towards certain danger until the depth drops to a safe minimum. You are at the edge of the channel, but you know that is where you are. You know in which directions must lie deeper and shallower water, but you hold your nerve and follow your contour line, keeping constant beneath you that safe quantity of water until you reach the haven.

N.J. HUMPHREY *(London)*

Without a paddle?

'I WILL YET,
TO SATISFY AND PLEASE MYSELF,
MAKE AN UTOPIA OF MINE OWN,
IN WHICH I WILL FREELY DOMINEER,
BUILD CITIES,
MAKE LAWS,
STATUTES,
AS I LIST MYSELF.
AND WHY MAY I NOT?'

ROBERT BURTON—(The Anatomy of Melancholy)

ANNOUNCEMENTS AND ADVERTISEMENTS—

Occasionally you may find dark coloured particles in the sugar, which are pieces of cane molasses.

They are entirely harmless and do not affect the flavour or cooking properties of the sugar.

Occasionally it may be necessary to replace a particular chocolate with another of equally high quality.

Sometimes you gotta hit a mule in the face with a piece of two by four to get its attention.

Never underestimate your enemy.

CLIVE WILLIAMSON *(Fenchurch)*

Sweet enough?

NOISE

Dear Enthusiast,

I would like to make a small clarification to my earlier letter to your gracious magazine. Noise, as we know well, is a big problem ; but so also, unfortunately, is silence. This question is further complicated by the issue of when exactly noise becomes silence, or vice versa, not to mention the question of what is not noise, and what is. Is noise better, or worse, when it is accompanied by light? Is it safer to precede light with noise, or is it more natural to precede noise with light? Can we risk the two appearing at exactly the same time? The history of civilisation has summed up this ambivalence in its sometimes screeching and sometimes subtle oscillation from noise to silence and back to noise.

My own long, unadvertised years of research into this subject have yielded, at first, the notion that, on the whole, human beings and scientists believe that silence is a much better thing. The results of a recent survey, for instance, showed that a full 93 per cent of respondents preferred it. The Zen masters, the Benedictine monks and the meditative gurus preferred it. What better–it was asked by one of the respondents to the survey, in favour of silence–than a quiet cowshed in the country (any country) with the susurrating grass and tinkling goat bells outside, the cow herself so content and serene and occupied in her cud-chewing that she finds no cause for mooing, when the only legitimate punctuation might be provided by the occasional defecative swish and plop? Surely this would be preferable to a jackhammer at 7 a.m.? Surely the moving image of the twin towers collapsing into rubble is more palatable–even more interesting–without sound? And yet, the answer is not so obvious. The cowshed serves as a pleasing dream-image but, as the conductors of the survey themselves noted, there was already a margin of error of 20–40 decibels in the respondents' descriptions of silence. Dead silence, when such a thing is possible for mammals with eardrums and circulatory systems, takes us to another kind of image altogether.

Thus while it may well be true, as one respondent noted, that 'silence is the spiritual knife which lays open our souls', it is not at all clear whether we really would like to be walking around from day to day with our souls open in this way. The evidence of our actions suggests the opposite. I, for one, admit that I have been so grateful for the obscuration of certain parts of certain phone conversations by helpful diesel trucks and angelic, low-flying aeroplanes that I have gone so far as to add my own coughs to the cacophony. And yet, noise, we know well, is more often best when it is organised, and organised by us, to our liking, and not by our neighbours, or by that fellow in the brand-new BMW.

Thankfully, recent technology has managed to address this conundrum with a rather clever solution : finding new ways to make noise, while at the same time finding new ways to cancel it. The silent aeroplane will be able to get much noisier when its wing-shaped fuselage will allow it to deflect its noise into the upper and not the lower atmosphere. Certain headphones now contain microphones that record sound and rotate it to create a sound-wave of an opposite polarity. Thus, it will be a matter of time before sound is completely liberated from vision, and from one's surroundings ; and even white noise will then be able to reveal itself more clearly in those many hues the prophetic sound engineers speak of and hear–the brown noise like a distant river, the grey noise like faint rain, the pink noise of simulated traffic, the violet noise like steam. While this freedom of sound-choice will no doubt present something of a challenge for collectively understood experience, it will surely be what we have been asking for.

Until then, what we are left with is an epic confrontation, still between Carnival and Lent as it were, and in the end it is our bodies and the bodies of our nations that are at stake. It is a question that is uppermost in my mind during these months in India, when every other day is a holiday, when wedding parties think nothing of spilling onto the street, when cars and buses chug into a provisional winter, when rival religions go into battle with the weapons of both noise and silence. India is a country that would desperately like to be quieter. Under relatively new noise pollution rules now being actually enforced, loudspeakers are banned within a 100-metre radius of courts, schools, hospitals, educational institutions and religious places, which is a strange and rather tall order. Noise levels are to be kept below 55 decibels in 'residential zones', where the normal reality hovers around 88.7 decibels. England, I suspect, is a country that secretly wishes to be much louder, louder even than its mythical lager louts ; England longs for an operatic voice.

Your humble correspondent,

VIVEK NARAYANAN *(New Delhi)*

Blah, blah, blah.

theenthusiast@theenthusiast.co.uk THE ENTHUSIAST, PO BOX 239, BANGOR, BT20 5YB

Technical Fault **Due to the technical fault, we had to cancel a number of things yesterday: the parade in your honour; the chat show; the witch-hunt.**

I spent most of the evening carrying bunting back to my garage and dismantling the floats. I was cross about the fault, naturally, but at least I was occupied.

Those who were forced to come back early from the witch-hunt were more vexed: not only did their new wooden torches go unlit, when they got in they found there wasn't even anything to watch on the telly.

Unfinished Business **The Italian writer Italo Calvino once said that he would like to edit a book of short stories comprising tales that were just one sentence, or a single line long. He claimed that the reason he had never done such a thing was that he had never found a story that could match the one by the Guatemalan writer Augusto Monterosso: 'Cuando desperto, el dinosauro todavia estaba alli.'**

(When he woke up, the dinosaur was still there.)

NICK PARKER *(London)*

Story to tell?

– PLEDGES –

YOUR FAMILY BETTER OFF
LIVING ABROAD

. . .

YOUR CHILD ACHIEVING
MORE MEGA-KILLS ON X-BOX

. . .

YOUR CHILDREN WITH THE BEST START
WHEN THE BARBARIANS GET OVER THE WALLS

. . .

YOUR FAMILY TREATED BETTER AND FASTER
BY A BETTER, FASTER, PEOPLE-TREATER

. . .

YOUR COMMUNITY SAFER
BY HIRING ITS OWN MILITIA

. . .

YOUR COUNTRY'S BORDERS PROTECTED
AS FAR AWAY AS IRAQ

- TRAVEL -

How to Cross a Bridge

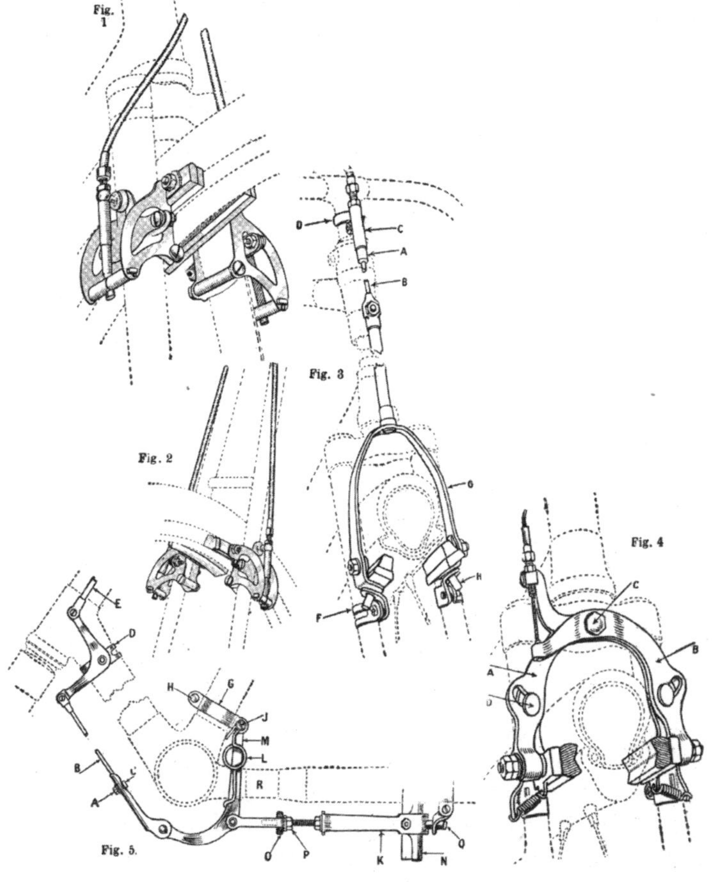

REMEMBER : a bridge is not a road. An obvious statement? Certainly not. There you are, perhaps on a Tuesday night. You are, let's say, in your automobile, returning from a dinner for seven (not eight, because someone's husband cried off) where you were careful not to have more than one glass of wine—this on account of the automobile—

but the bridge you're about to cross has no toll and so, as you drive, you are still wondering what your host's cousin meant when she said : *only the child understands the loneliness of its parents.*

Because of this, you don't notice the bridge. Oil smoothes the mechanism of your vehicle, the windows are rolled right up and you sail up over the river and away from the island with no regard at all for any of these words : suspension, tension, compression.

That night, however, something wakes you. Your feet are hot and your head is cold. You don't hear a siren and there are no dogs barking but the lids of your eyes are parted and you watch the wall, barred with simmering light from a streetlamp threading through the Venetian blind. Why had you never noticed you were right at the foot of that bridge?

Don't look at your watch. It is midnight, or three o'clock in the morning. Don't try to catch your reflection in the hall mirror as you leave the house (your socks don't match, and maybe neither do your shoes) because you can't be sure what you'll see. Walk down the stairs, keeping your feet an inch in the air above each tread, and once outside keep the closed stone arches on your right.

You understand that this is the anchorage : allow your feet to touch the ground.

Narrow steps lead you to a walkway which rises above where the motor traffic—even at this hour, whatever hour it actually is—runs beneath. The walkway is of wood. Put one foot in front of the other. Walk in a straight line.

Below the roadway, the walkway, around the foot of the towers, is the river, nearly black but slicked in streaks with the white light that falls from the bridge. You know what you have to do.

Four steel cables carry the span. Each cable made from strands of wire laid parallel and then bound hard, clamped and bolted and held. Did you know this? As soon as you set your palm against the cold metal you remembered the story you'd been told about a decision cut through air and over water, passed up from the beginning (a young man in a soft felt hat standing at a ferry slip, a cigar in his hand that's about to go out and suddenly distracted by the thought of his wife's neck, the hollow below the blade of her shoulder) into the future (where you'll stand shortly, on the other side, wondering if you can ever turn back).

Take four steps towards the stone towers whose eyes or mouths drag you forwards, and now the great cable is at the level of your hip, your elbow, your shoulder, your nose. No one sits on this unpainted bench, or that one either, but do not stop : continue on towards where narrower cables—wires twisted around each other like the ropes they remember they once were—drop vertically to the bridge floor.

There are lights ahead and lights behind, two cities, or one, it doesn't matter because *only the child understands the loneliness of its parents*. Yes, all that was a long time ago : the iron bars that kept you out of the garden, the thick hot air that fed the white embers burning below the river's mud, the crucible that held the molten tongue of the spool. One tower stands on rock and the other on sand : the bridge is built from belief.

Take the rope in your hands, the metal rope. Your feet hold the upward curve of the walk and your spine echoes the cable's curve. The rope travels through your skin, up through the small bones that fan between your fingers, the joint of your wrist, the two curved bones of your forearm, your collarbone, your breastbone, your heart. It's getting warmer now, what's in your grasp, the heat of blood or milk, and the atoms that separate skin from steel, vibrate and dissolve. Which of you is alive?

1,595 feet, six inches : the main span. *Five feet, six inches : the breadth of your arms, spread wide, middle finger tip to middle finger tip*. 276 feet, six inches : the height of the towers. *Three years, two months, seven days, three hours and fourteen and a half minutes : the length of time it took you to understand that what disappears, does not*. 119 feet, three inches : the clear height in the centre of the river span above high water. *Seven : how old you were when you first saw a hawk*. 23 tons : the weight of each anchor plate. *Twenty five : a quarter of everything, of course*. 15 3/4 inches : diameter of each of the four main cables. *One hundred and twenty-nine hours, forty minutes, twelve seconds : total number of hours you will spend dreaming of rooms whose walls don't meet at their corners*. Nineteen strands in each cable ; each strand made from 5,434 wires ; 3,515 miles of wire in each cable. *Thirty-seven : your age now*.

Suspension, tension, compression. There are no answers ; there are only replies. Keep walking. This is the recommended method for crossing a bridge.

EMILY WARREN *(London)* *Which bridge do you like?*

Six recipes from the back of the larder

POLENTA WITH CHEESE

PUT SPOONFULS of polenta all over a dish, grate cheese over, then stew little bits of butter (dobs not flecks), pepper, and salt, then another layer of polenta, and so on till you have enough. Only you will be able to say when you have enough. You might want to go on past experience. Brown it over the fire, or not, as you choose. In place of butter you may put gravy, either of mushrooms or meat. If not meat, perhaps a vegetable bouillon.

HOMMONY

BOIL ONE-THIRD of a pound of meal – you will find a packet of meal at the back of the store cupboard, next to the dried chick-peas and the cracked lentils; pay no regard to the date of purchase – in enough water to cover it, for twenty minutes, or until all the water is wasted; it must be like a thick paste – you might compare porridge, or a glutinous soup; plaster of Paris is a bad analogy. Put a piece of butter the size of a walnut – this is an approximate measure; think of a large dob – into a vegetable dish. Pour in the hommony, and serve it mashed, like turnips. Dip your spoon in the middle, when you help it. There are other ways of cooking hommony, but I am not prepared to give directions for them. Warning: this meal is hot.

A NICE PUDDING

THIS DISH is made like Ground Rice. Mix two ounces of meal smooth with half a pint of cold milk, and pour over it three half pints of new milk scalded, stir it over the fire till it thickens: let it cool, then add four eggs well beaten, sugar, nutmeg, and a spoonful of orange-flower water, beat it, and pour it into a dish with a paste border. Bake it half an hour. Or, adding two more eggs, this may be boiled in a basin, an hour. This may of course be

Salty enough for you?

theenthusiast@theenthusiast.co.uk

The Enthusiast, PO Box 239,
BANGOR BT20 5YB

flavoured in any way you choose. Use your discretion. Try cinnamon, maybe, or extract of lime. If it doesn't work throw the whole sorry mess away. There are, after all, more eggs.

DUMPLINGS

THESE ARE made of meal wet up with water or milk, and boiled in a cloth, to eat with bacon or pork; and I think would not be objected to in the farm-houses of those counties where dumplings prevail. Roughly speaking dumplings prevail in Yorkshire (South and West Ridings), Nottinghamshire, Co. Durham, Shropshire, Lincolnshire and parts of Suffolk. The jury is still out on Avon and Greater Manchester. Middlesex, as in all things, is a kettle of fish.

JOHNNY CAKE

THIS IS made in the same manner as ash-cake, and baked before the fire, first on one-side, and then on the other. There are no restrictions as to the sequence of sides, although here also one might refer to the manner of ash-cake.

MUSH

THIS MUSH IS, in fact, porridge, and like the latter is made thick or thin, as you like. Here again you might want to exercise your discretion. In this, as in all things, practice will make perfect. I do it as follows: having five pints of water or milk, whichever you prefer, boiling fast on the fire – think not to look away for a moment, because before you know it you have boiled too fast – put in a small teaspoonful of salt, and while you keep stirring with your right hand, drop gently from your left hand, and by degrees, one pound of meal. Equally stir with your left, and drop with your right. On no account here should you pat your stomach. Let it boil twenty minutes, stirring well all the time or it will be lumpy; a stick is best. [A stick is always best when it comes to mush. Beat hard until the mush acquires an edge. This will take longer in some climates than others. Britain, for instance, requires more beating than some parts of America, though less than large tracts of mainland Europe.] If the meal be fine, then it is better to wet it up with cold water into a smooth batter first, and stir that into the boiling water; but you must stir it all the time it is boiling, and in this case as well as in the other. Upon beating and boiling, ventilation is advised.

W.F. HILL *(Eversley)*

– CORRECTIONS AND CLARIFICATIONS –

SORRY, but like you we've been so busy recently – war, famines, environmental disasters – we haven't had time for anything, nothing at all, not even shame, despair or regret. Nonetheless, for the sake of clarity, regarding recent errors : well, we hear what you're saying, but we'll stick with what we've got, thank you very much ; and yes, you *can* avoid London, it's easy, just don't go there in the first place ; and yes, it was nice of you to ask, but no, thanks, we have no desire to attend your prestigious event ; and, anyway, we have nothing to wear, only odd cloth and fragments ; and certainly, we're prepared to swear on a stack of Bibles that this is what we mean; and for those many of you who seem to have forgotten, there is a difference between candid feedback and abuse. And also, finally, and our last word on this matter – we beg to differ with your old English teacher and your friends in the pub – the commonest fault among amateurs is not in intention, attitude, mindset, tone, pitch or clever typographical layout, it's in *content.*

Any errors?

---

theenthusiast@theenthusiast.co.uk THE ENTHUSIAST, PO BOX 239, BANGOR, BT20 5YB

'IT BELONGS TO MEN OF SLAVISH PRINCIPLES TO AFFECT A SUPERIORITY OVER THE VULGAR, AND TO DESPISE THE MULTITUDE. THE LOVERS OF MANKIND RESPECT AND HONOUR OUR CONVENTIONS AND SOCIETIES OF MEN.'

EARL OF SHAFTESBURY—(Characteristics of Men, Manners, Opinions, Times)

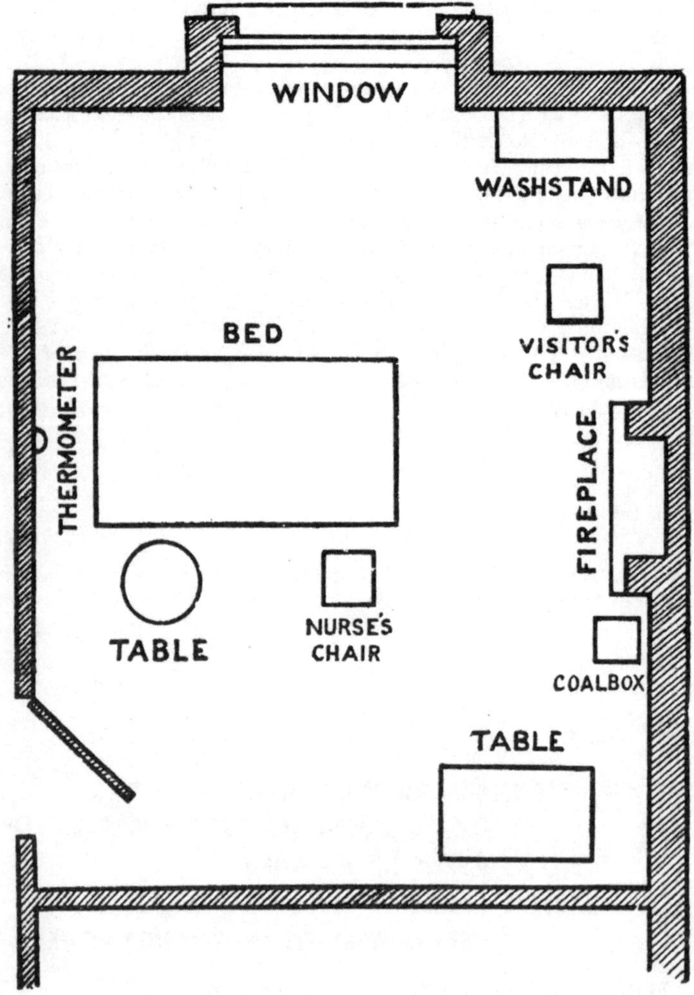
WINDOW
WASHSTAND
VISITOR'S
CHAIR
BED
THERMOMETER
FIREPLACE
TABLE
NURSE'S
CHAIR
COALBOX
TABLE

– ANNOUNCEMENTS AND ADVERTISEMENTS –

WHY NOT BE AN AUTHOR?

AS AN AUTHOR, you can earn millions of pounds and become a literary colossus in your spare time, penning the kind of exquisitely structured, richly charactered, universally themed mega-tomes that publishers and moral beings want. Trillions of euros sloosh around the aqueducts of Bookland. Earning your share whilst thinking and writing about the human condition can be fun.

To help you become a critically lauded author of international renown we will send you our pukka LearnPak™, devised by established geniuses and offering individually tailored tutoring from figures who tower in their fields. You are shown how to steal ideas, how to underachieve through character weakness, how to hold controversial opinions and how to deliver the all-important prizewinner's speech. Whether your aim is mainstream mega-sales or edgier-than-thou cult status, this is the course for you ... because it's good and professional and all that.

The course is perfect for beginners. You don't need any experience of writing (or indeed of life), you merely think your stuff onto the screen using BrainSoft™*, which is like information technology. There is no pressure, there are no time limits, which encourages creativity and discourages refund claims. So confident are we that the course is FoolProof™ that we offer you a Guarantee™ – if you don't receive an obscenity of an advance based on two and a half chapters and the say-so of a booze-ruddy agent within hours of beginning the course, we promise to return a percentage of your fee, should your court action prove successful.

Fill in the coupon below like the lexical heavyweight you are and send it to the Authors' Association.

NAME ....

NOM DE PLUME ....

ALIAS ....

BANK DETAILS ....

PAGER ....

(*cost of software and DumpPod™ not included)

– ADVERTISEMENT (CONT.) –

COURSE FEATURES

- **515 informative modules**
- **29 E-Z Assemble™ FactPads™**
- **ThoughtThru™ study programme**
- **International Support™ call centre**
- **4 free characters (including optional anti-hero or sorceress)**
- **How to write stuff down**
- **How to decide it's garbage and waste the day watching the History Channel**
- **How to start again**
- **How to show it to some guy**
- **How to deal with instant adoration from the literary élite**

* * * * *

'Within hours of starting the course I received $48,000 for some polishing I did on a script Pixar were developing. In the end they used like two lines. I can't remember the name of the film. But it was cool staying in the Beverly Wilshire for a month. That's some bona fortuna!'

KEN DEIGHTON, *Skelmersdale*

'My debut novel has shaken the goddamn literary establishment to its core! I redefined the possibilities of fiction beyond the wildest dreams of any other living writer. My name will live forever. And all thanks to the correspondence course from the Authors' Association.'

DAVE BINCHY, *Bracknell*

'Before I studied with the Authors' Association I was an itinerant drug addict and petty thief. I will remain forever indebted to the tutor whose bile-rich, personalised attacks encouraged me to write the teen slush that's paid for this tasty set of gold sovereign rings. Read that!'

GILL BRYSON, *Thurrock*

- HEALTH -

SELF-DOUBT

DO YOU EVER DOUBT YOURSELF? Is self-doubt prudent? Do you know of anybody who doesn't doubt himself enough? Should leaders doubt themselves? Is your employer ever in doubt? Is doubt a precondition for a robust faith?

In an occasional series of interviewers with trades-people and professionals—teachers, plasterers, politicians, artists, plumbers, carers, probation officers, and taxi-drivers—*The Enthusiast* asks, 'How do you handle self-doubt?'

This interview: screenwriters

'*I am my toughest critic ... and that's terrible.* It's good because it means that I care about my work but at the same time it creates a lot of insecurities. Then I find myself rewriting a stupid scene for the thousandth time and I take twenty days to do it. I hate that. But then some days I write twenty pages and that's it, I don't question it. I don't like people who are very receptive towards my work, because it doesn't help me. When I finish something I usually give it to my wife and to Alfonso. That's because they are both so critical. I have that deal with my brother. If I am giving him something to read he has to tell me the truth about what he thinks.'

'*Doubting yourself as a screenwriter would be like doubting yourself as a roller-blader.* Who cares, really? I'm certainly not going to beat myself up about it. I find that certain things can be going badly and not be coming out well but I just don't think it's going to be that difficult to sort it all out. So I guess the way we get past it is like extreme arrogance in a way because we feel we understand as well as anybody else what has to be done to make something work well in a screenplay. I've had a lot of doubts about myself as a filmmaker because you're in a world of infinite possibilities and it's terrifying and gut-wrenching and then you have to take a deep breath and jump ... But I don't feel like screenwriting is brain surgery.'

'*I don't know how you handle it because it is a constant thing.* I think what I always try to do is say to myself, "How did I feel about this last one when I was around this point, was I feeling good?" The answer to that is usually, "No, you were feeling terrible. You didn't even know that you wanted to make the movie." Usually I ask somebody else to remind me because I have a mental block and it always seems like it was going better on the last one. There are always times when you don't know if it's a movie. The thing we are on now is as much a movie-movie as anything, and up until six weeks ago I just wasn't sure if we were on the right track at all and somehow we turned a corner and got confident about it.'

'*Oh yeah, self-doubt is a daily exercise and that's why you need to be passionate about the material.* You'll wake up many mornings over those two or three years and you'll be totally at a loss as to why you're doing this, what is the purpose. And you have to hate your project.

10. Hare. 11. Teddy Bear. 12. Ox. 13. Dog.

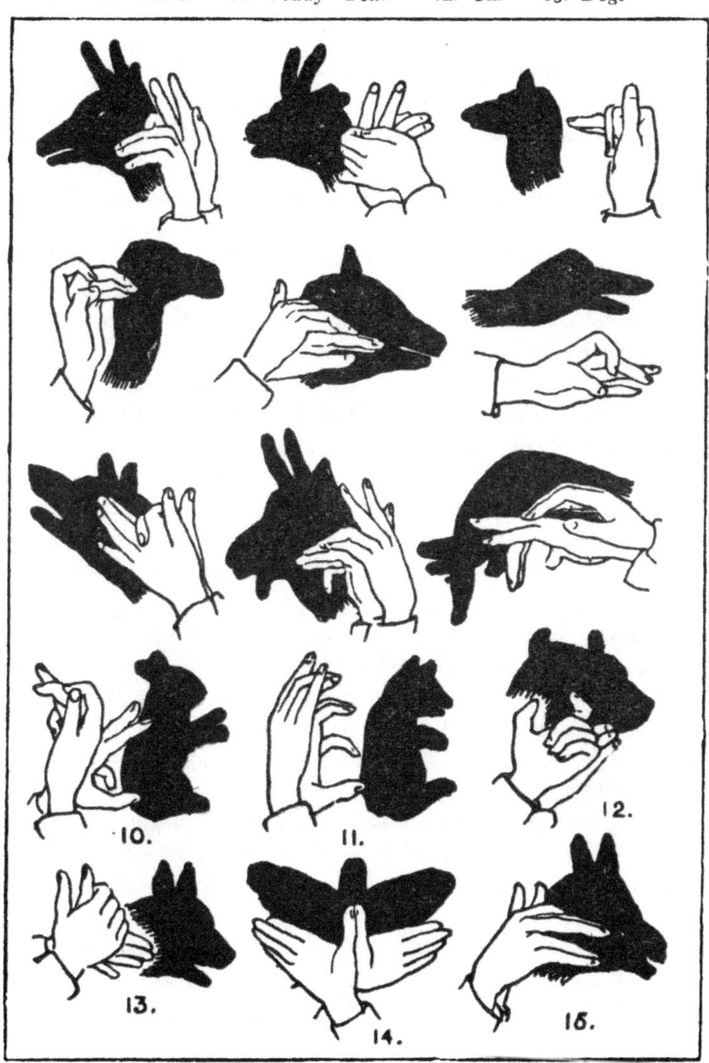

14. Butterfly. 15. Donkey.

My dad used to say, "A man without doubt is a man without wisdom." You have to constantly keep doubting yourself because otherwise you'll get cocky and that's what destroys you.'

'*I think you deal with it when you're early in your career just by the sheer energy and determination you have to make it ; and if you allow yourself to be side-tracked by self-doubt at that stage you'll basically fall by the wayside and cease to produce.* You've got to just keep on working even though you know the work is not good enough, but you keep on working because you have no choice, because you're driven, or whatever. And then later on you gain a confidence that enables you, when you have an inability to solve a problem, to get a story on its feet, get a character to come to life. You have the confidence born of experience that you've been in this mess before, and that just by staying at your table, staring at it and trying to make an idea come to you, if you stick with it long enough you'll solve the problem—because your own history has told you that.'

'*It's hell for me usually because of self-doubt.* I try to trick myself. What gets in the way for me is a very strong inner critic and powerful, powerful feelings of self-doubt and voices that constantly identify me as a fraud and inadequate to the task. So what I do is I try very hard to mute the voices as much as I can. I know that they'll never go away but I can make them like the radio in the next room where you can hear them but they're not bothering you. They're there and I'm aware of them but I have some sort of arrangement with them. The best writing is also subconscious, where you don't know that you're doing it and you don't realise you've done it. That's a few seconds and the rest of the week is using the other half of your brain manipulating what you've come up with in those few seconds. The only way you can get to those subconscious places is by having a sense of play ; it should always feel like play. That's how I try to do it. If I'm not having fun, it's wrong. Sometimes it's not fun but even when you're under a lot of pressure, you need to try and have fun and try to be excited and exhilarated and that's the hard part.'

'*I go through that all the time.* It is always difficult. I think there are two kinds of self-doubt. One is a kind of constructive self-doubt, that is a self-doubt when you are self-critical—"There is something wrong but I am going to fix it." That can be a very nice and interesting feeling because that is a feeling that gives birth to new ideas like "I am going to change this friend into a mother." But when you're feeling "This is bad and I don't know how to fix it", that is terrible. The problem is that it is like a virus that spreads into everything that you have written. Sometimes I can be sitting there, writing, and I can think "This dialogue is so crappy." Then later I might go further "Not only is this dialogue crappy, it is a symptom of everything I have ever written." So suddenly it is like "I am nothing and I have written nothing in my life." That's terrible. But on the other hand you have to go through a depression to get out and go through to the other side.'

'*I think, when it happens, and it happens a lot, I think it's right to go on, not to stop.* Sometimes it happens because it doesn't work and you are very slow, and of course you want to call somebody or go out, so you do. And then after a few days of writing a lot you are very slow because you're not happy with what you're writing. I just try to go on, if I'm writing a sequence and I don't like it, I don't like the way they're talking, what's going on, then I try to keep writing even when I don't like it. To go forward and then maybe four sequences later it will become nice again.'

'*I slept a lot . . . I sometimes wonder if all writers have the same dysfunctional patterns.* But I was like a narcoleptic, I slept so much, it was hard to sit at my desk. I had a couple of friends I would call, who were filmmakers who I would melt down with. You really want to know a typical day? It's like the office never closes, right? So the minute you get up you're like "Fuck, I've got to go back to that fucking script", like there's this monkey on your back. So you get up at the crack of dawn and you make coffee, go back into your bedroom and read the *New York Times*—and that's the most beautiful period of the day. You're entitled to have that coffee, you're entitled to read your copy of the *Times*.'

KEVIN CONROY SCOTT *(Clapham)*, WITH THANKS TO CARLOS CUARON, CHRIS WEITZ, WES ANDERSON, DARREN ARONOFSKY, PATRICK MCGRATH, SCOTT FRANK, LUKAS MODDYSSON, FERNANDO LEÓN DE ARANOA, LISA CHOLODENKO.

What are you entitled to?

theenthusiast@theenthusiast.co.uk THE ENTHUSIAST, PO BOX 239, BANGOR, BT20 5YB

- TRAVEL -

Nepal

Men from the Yalabang monastery were already astir. The morning had begun to tease us mischievously through a little window of the building. Today, again, we had to walk.

The lama in the monastery was Rangrikjee's distant *mama (maternal uncle)*, and therefore we too addressed him as *mama*. Rangrikjee himself was a respectable *autari* lama. His father was a learned and revered *autari* lama. Naturally we were treated well because Rangrikjee was in our company. But it would be unfair to say that the lama had been so hospitable and helpful to us just for that. It is lama culture to help, love and treat their guests cordially.

I had a wrong notion about lamas when I was young. I was terrified and would maintain a safe distance from them, or run away. I used to take lamas to be cruel and heartless. Though that notion had been erased by and by, I think it had still not completely been washed away. That too is now wiped away. A profound affection and reverence for them arose in me — a happy outcome of my walk into the Himalayas.

But time was secretly slipping away. We tried to bid farewell to *mama* and others at the monastery. But *mama* was not going to let go of us so easily. A man of heart as large as the earth, his love was as large as the blues. He insisted we eat with him. We had *khura* with radish chutney. Boundless satisfaction and joy spread over *mama*'s face.

Before we left, *mama* unlocked the monastery gate. We took off our shoes and entered. There was a large hall for worship, prayer and hymns, and a huge statue of Lord Buddha meditating on top of a slightly elevated place right in front. Beneath it oil lamps were burning and looked like clusters of twinkling stars. My eyes felt everything. I can't say what, but an inexplicable emotion surged in me when I stood in front of the statue. Slowly I bowed deeply. Laden with reverence, I touched the feet of Lord Buddha and swam into the boundless sea of peace and satisfaction. I was enchanted by the brilliance of spotless beauty and charm. Rangrikjee took my photograph. I took his.

And so we left, walking along the narrow path that passed by the yard of the monastery and disappeared into the south. Soon this joined a wider path. We followed this new path downhill for almost half an hour, to reach a small Bhote village named Yangar. Green fields, green trees, green apple trees: Yangar was well into its youth. Happily, also, there was a hydroelectric powerhouse there. Some women were washing clothes in the clear water that came out of the powerhouse, and last night Yalabang had been swollen with pride with the electric lights produced here. How nice it would be if small projects like this were launched at other places also! Better still if the government itself launched them. That way, perhaps, the autocracy of darkness would fade from other villages too, and the tragic story of poor people searching for their uncertain future in the dim light of diyalo lamps would come to an end!

Rajnarayanjee rested himself on a stone near the water, his bag on the ground. I followed suit. Rangrikjee and the helper soon arrived. They wished to go on slowly, leaving us behind, but my eyes were fixed on the red apples hanging thickly in a green tree. A bunch of local kids swarmed around us. Dressed in dirty and worn-out clothes, they had some textbooks and notebooks with them. They looked at us quizzically. I talked to one of them. He said they went to the school at Yalabang. Rajnarayanjee asked one of the boys to call the owner of the apple garden. We bought the apples for six rupees. Dogs started barking loudly at us from all directions.

Again our path ran along the banks of the Karnali river. Now the way was level, now it ran steep down to the banks of the Karnali. Soon it would climb steep up to the chest of the Himalaya. In Kathmandu at times, when I would feel bored to death, or mused on the meaninglessness of life, or was wrapped up in despair, I would have a feeling of death. The meaninglessness of life pushed me near death and death would be a kind of music. I was, I thought, ready to die. But life is dear to a man. Man is in fact in love with life. Man has got a life to love and live through. Withdrawing under the shade of a tree, I caressed my life. It held me tight and I grew careful. During the breathtaking climb uphill, I remained on guard all the time. For the first time I was in love with life.

BHISMA UPRETI *(Kathmandu)*

Translated by MUKUL DAHAL and DINESH PAUDEL

In love with life?

theenthusiast@theenthusiast.co.uk
THE ENTHUSIAST, PO BOX 239, BANGOR, BT20 5YB

– ADVICE –

Marry a plumber.

LYNN ABBOTT *(Colchester)*

In the garden, remember, green is a colour.

JESSICA CASSAVA *(Kingston-upon-Thames)*

Never shit on a shamrock.

MALISE O'CONNOR *(Belfast)*

Note: all buses cover their routes in both directions. Eventually.

ARTHUR BUTCHER *(Leytonstone)*

Always make time for tiramisu.

MARTIN JONES *(Sunderland)*

Beat the eggwhites, not the bowl.

GEORGE LAPP *(Selkirk)*

Dress to suit your figure.

J. SZILAND *(Manchester)*

Take no notice of what the others say: kindness is a big deal.

VICKIE WESLEY *(Lewisham)*

Do not slump, or eat wet food. Answer not your calls. Wear shoes. Wear no hat-pins with unprotected points. Engage in no rough-play.

A CONCERNED MOTORIST *(Chepstow)*

You do what?

Electricity

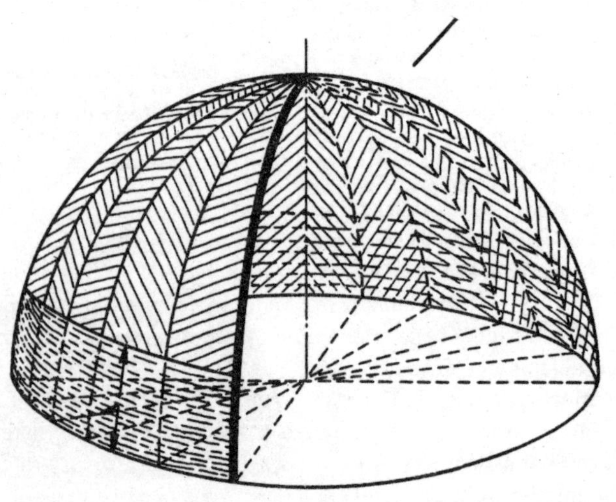

Fig. 1.

WHEN, IN 1767, Joseph Priestley (1733–1804) came to write his *History and Present State of Electricity*, it seemed to him that a boundless opportunity was opening up for mankind. Here was a power whose application might be endless ; a force that might generate a thousand inventions. Priestley himself was a radical in politics, religion and in natural philosophy : he advocated revolution ; was one of the original members of the Unitarian Society ; and discovered oxygen, hydrochloric acid, nitric oxide, and sulphur dioxide, among other gases. *He is a quintessential figure of the late English enlightenment ; a polymath ; a ceaseless experimenter ; a tester of received opinions.*

In the summer of 1765, his work on the nature of electricity led him to perform a series of experiments on the effects of electrical current on animals. The results were, in every sense, explosive. That someone so fundamentally humane as Priestley could have been led into the cruelties practised here is a psychological curiosity that would not have surprised his conservative critics. In *A Letter to a Noble Lord*, Edmund Burke bitterly attacked the mathematicians and chemists of the radical left ; their coldly experimental attitude to life had deprived them of the unexamined feelings and customs that were the moral supports of the civilised world.

In reading of Priestley's gruesome gathering of scientific knowledge, we might be reminded of Samuel Johnson's magnificent retort to Soame Jenyns's *A Free Inquiry into the Nature and Origin of Evil*, published in 1757, only some ten years before Priestley began his summer experiments. Jenyns had coolly argued that perhaps our sufferings happen for some higher beings' pleasure or utility. The implications of this statement roused Johnson to majestic disdain: 'He might have shown that these *hunters, whose game is man* have many sports analogous to our own. As we drown whelps and kittens, they amuse themselves now and then with sinking a ship ... As we shoot a bird flying, they take a man in the midst of his business or pleasure, and knock him down with an apoplexy. Some of them, perhaps, are virtuosi, and delight in the operations of an asthma, as a human philosopher in the effects of the air pump. To swell a man with a tympany is as good sport as to blow a frog.' Priestley stands here at one crux of our relationship with animals, caught between the requirements of knowledge and the desire for compassion.

* * *

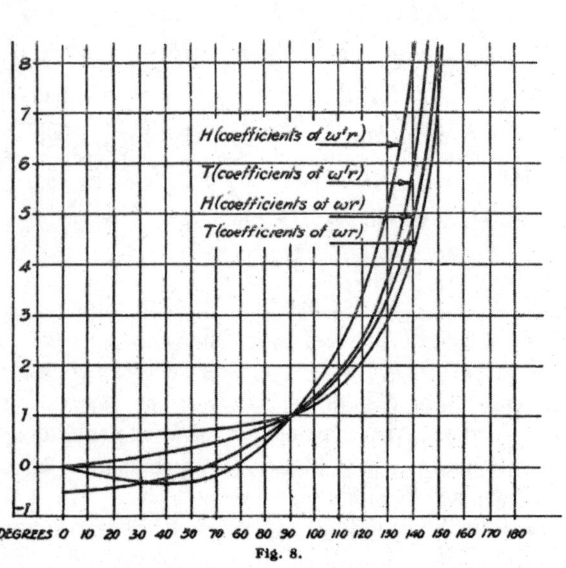

Fig. 8.

* * *

As I have constructed an electrical battery of considerably greater force than any other that I have yet heard of, and as I have sometimes exposed animals to the shock of it, and have particularly attended to several circumstances, which have been overlooked, or misapprehended by others ; it may not be improper to relate a few of the cases, in which the facts were, in any respect, new, or worth notice.

Enteric
(Typhoid)
Notes of Case
Name Wm. Anon
Age 221 yrs.
Diet Liquid
Case Book No. 1.

June the 4th. I killed a rat with the discharge of two jars, each containing three square feet of coated glass. The animal died immediately, after being universally convulsed, at the instant of the stroke. After some time, it was carefully dissected ; but there was no internal injury perceived, particularly no extravasation, either in the abdomen, thorax, or brain.

June the 19th. I killed a pretty large kitten with the discharge of a battery of thirty-three square feet ; but no other effect was observed, except that a red spot was found on the pericranium, where the fire entered. I endeavoured to bring it to life, by distending the lungs, blowing with a quill into the trachea, but to no purpose. The heart beat a short time after the stroke, but respiration ceased immediately.

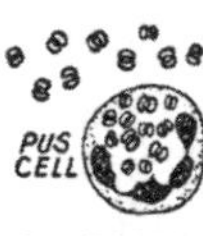

GONOCOCCI

ANTHRAX BACILLI

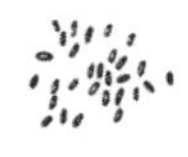
INFLUENZA BACILLI

June the 21st. I killed a small field-mouse with the discharge of a battery of thirty-six square feet, but no other effect was perceived, except that the hair of the forehead was singed, and in part torn off. There was no extravasation anywhere, though the animal was so small, and the force with which it was killed was so great. This fact, and many others of a similar nature, make me suspect some mistake, in cases where larger animals are said to have had all their blood vessels burst by a much inferior force.

In all the accounts that I have met with of animals killed by electric shock, the victims were either small quadrupeds, or fowls ; and they are all represented as killed so suddenly, that it could not be seen how they were affected previous to their expiration. In some of my experiments, the great force of my battery has afforded me a pretty fair opportunity of observing in what manner the animal system is affected by the electric shock, the animals which I have exposed it to being pretty large ; so that a better judgement may be formed of their sensations, and consequently of the immediate cause of their death, by external signs. I do not pretend to draw any conclusion myself from the following facts. I have only noted them as carefully as I could for the use of physicians and anatomists.

June the 26th. I discharged a battery of thirty-eight square feet of coated glass, through the head, and out at the tail of a *full grown cat*, three or four years old. At that instant, she was violently convulsed all over. After a short respite, there came on smaller convulsions, in various muscles, particularly on the sides ; which terminated in a violent convulsive respiration, attended with a rattling in the throat. This continued five minutes, without any motion that could be called breathing, but was succeeded by an exceeding quick respiration, which continued near half an hour. Towards the end of this time, she was able to move her head, and fore feet, so as to push herself backwards on the floor ; but she was not able to move her hind feet in the least, notwithstanding the shock had not passed through them. While she continued in this condition, I gave her a second stroke, which was attended, as before, with the violent convulsion, the short respite, and the convulsive respiration ; in which, after continuing about a minute, she died.

Being willing to try, for once, the effect of a much greater shock than that which killed the cat upon a large animal, I gave an explosion of sixty-two square feet of coated glass to a dog the size of a common cur. The moment he was struck, which was on the head (but, not having a very good light, I could not tell exactly where) all his limbs were extended, he fell backwards, and lay without any motion, or sign of life for about a minute. Then followed convulsions, but not very violent, in all his limbs ; and after that a convulsive respiration, attended with a small rattling in the throat. In about four minutes from the time that he was struck, he was able to move, though he did not offer to walk till about half an hour after ; in all which time, he kept discharging a great quantity of saliva ; and there was also a great flux of rheum from his eyes, on which he kept putting his feet ; though in other respects he lay perfectly listless. He never opened his eyes all the evening in which he was struck, and the next morning he appeared to be quite blind, though seemingly well in every other respect.

Having dispatched the dog, by shooting him through the hinder part of his head, I examined one of his eyes (both of which had an uniform blueish cast, like a film over the pupil) and found all the three

ERB

No.	Hyp. Log.	No.	Hyp. Log.	No.	Hyp. Log.	No.	Hyp. Log.
			42°				
			41°				
			40°				
			39°				
				8·75			
				8·90			
			Temperature (Centigrade)	9·00			
				9·10			
			38°	9·15			
				9·20			
				9·25			
				9·30			
				9·35			
			37°				
			36°				
			35°				

humours perfectly transparent, and, as far as could be judged, in their right state ; but the *cornea* was throughout white and opaque, like a bit of gristle, and remarkably thick.

Before this experiment, I had imagined, that animals struck blind by lightning had probably a *gutta serena*, on account of the concussion which is seemingly given to the nervous system by the electric shock ; whereas this case was evidently an inflammation, occasioned by the explosion being made so near the eyes, terminating in a species of the *albugo* ; but which I suppose would have been incurable. One of the eyes of this dog was affected a little more than the other ; owing, probably, to the stroke being made a little nearer to one eye than the other. I intended to give the stroke about an inch above the eyes.

'ARE YOU NOT CARRIED
OUT OF YOURSELF, AND
DOES NOT YOUR SOUL
IN AN ECSTASY
SEEM TO BE AMONG THE
PERSONS OR PLACES
OF WHICH
YOU ARE SPEAKING,
WHETHER THEY ARE
IN ITHACA OR IN TROY
OR WHATEVER MAY BE THE
SCENE OF THE POEM.'

PLATO—(Ion)

In order to ascertain the effects of electricity on an animal body, I, after this, began a course of experiments on the conducting power of its constituent parts ; and for some time imagined that a piece of spinal marrow of an ox conducted sensibly worse than the muscular flesh ; but after a great number of trials with pieces of spinal marrow from various animals, and pieces of muscular flesh, of the same size and form, and in various states of moisture and dryness, I gave up that opinion as fallacious ; but I cannot help wishing the experiments were resumed with some more accurate measure of conducting power than has yet been contrived.

Being willing to observe, if possible, the immediate effect of the electric shock on the heart and lungs of animals, I gave, on June the 5th, a shock from six square feet to a frog, in which the thorax had previously been laid open, so that the pulsation of the heart might be seen. Upon receiving the stroke, the lungs were instantly inflated ; and, together with the other contents of the thorax, thrown quite out of the body. The heart, however, continued to beat, though very languidly, and there was no other sign of life for about ten minutes. After that, a motion was first perceived under its jaws ; which was propagated, by degrees, to the muscles of the sides ; and at last the creature seemed as if it would have come to life, if it had not been so much mangled. The stroke entered the head, and went out at the hind feet.

June the 6th. I discharged a battery of thirty-three square feet through the head and whole extended body of another frog. Immediately upon receiving the stroke, there was, as it were, a momentary distention of all the muscles of the body, and it remained shrivelled up in a most surprising manner. For about five minutes there appeared no sign of life, and the pulsation of the heart could not be felt with the finger. But afterwards, there first appeared a motion under the jaws, then all along the sides, attended with convulsive motions of the other parts, and in about an hour it became, to all appearances, as well as ever.

The same day, I gave the same stroke to two other frogs. They were affected in the same manner, and perfectly recovered in less than three hours.

These facts surprised me very much. I attribute the recovery of the frogs partly to the moisture, which always seems to cover their body, and which might transmit a good part of the shock ; and partly to that provision in their constitution, whereby they can subsist a long time without breathing. To ascertain this, I would have given the shock to toads, serpents, fishes, &c. and various other exanguious animals, but I had not an opportunity. Besides, it is paying dear for philosophical discoveries, to purchase them at the expense of humanity.

(From Joseph Priestley, *The History and Present State of Electricity, with Original Experiments*. Fourth Edition. London, 1775: 597–601.)

MICHAEL NEWTON *(Berlin)*

Galvanise!

theenthusiast@theenthusiast.co.uk

THE ENTHUSIAST, PO BOX 239, BANGOR, BT20 5YB

- WHAT I BELIEVE -

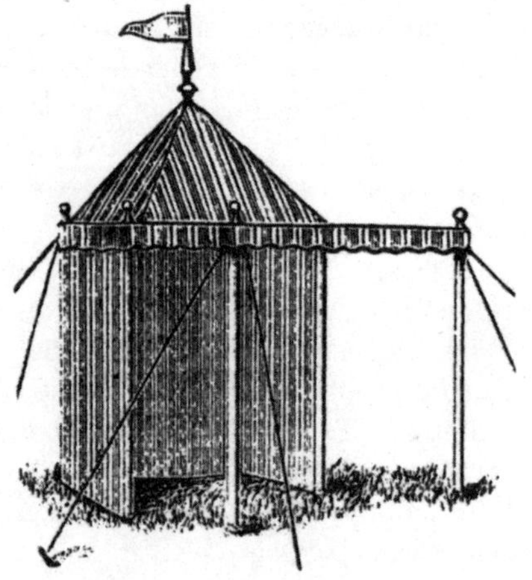

I believe there is a back door with a latch,
by which persons may let themselves in.

T.J. PRESS *(Norwich)*

Under the mat?

Gadgets

We live in difficult times. We have shoe bombs and reality TV, the worldwide web and a worldwide war. So we need new gadgets, and Chinese manufacturing needs us to need them now.

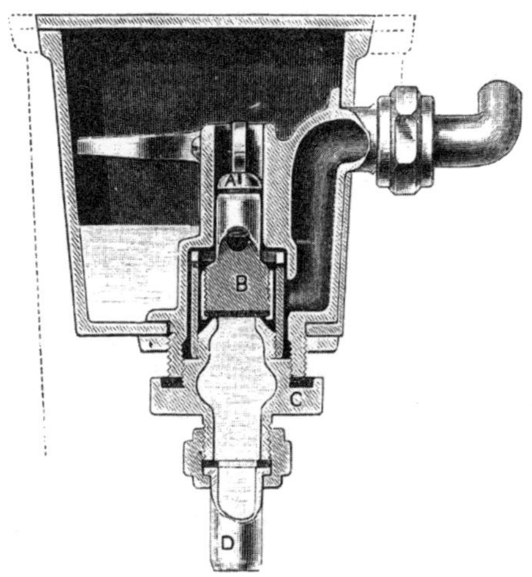

QXZ—

If you've been looking for a way to upgrade your *QXZ*, look no further. Axel Head of Norfolk Technologies are bringing out a *QXZ* that will definitely pomp your ride. The anti-vibration programme is second to none and the handgrip shape is the kind of evolutionary hyper-leap that you thought only happened on the Galapagos Islands. The BAM cell has the kind of storage that would shame the Trojan Horse, and the ultra-designer venting means that a midnight overheat is nowhere near the worry it once was. There are, of course, some down-downs. For no reason it makes your knees hurt after about five hours, the skull and cross-bones motif is a bit rubbish and it's not quite as portable as the ads would have you believe. But for that price—snap it up!

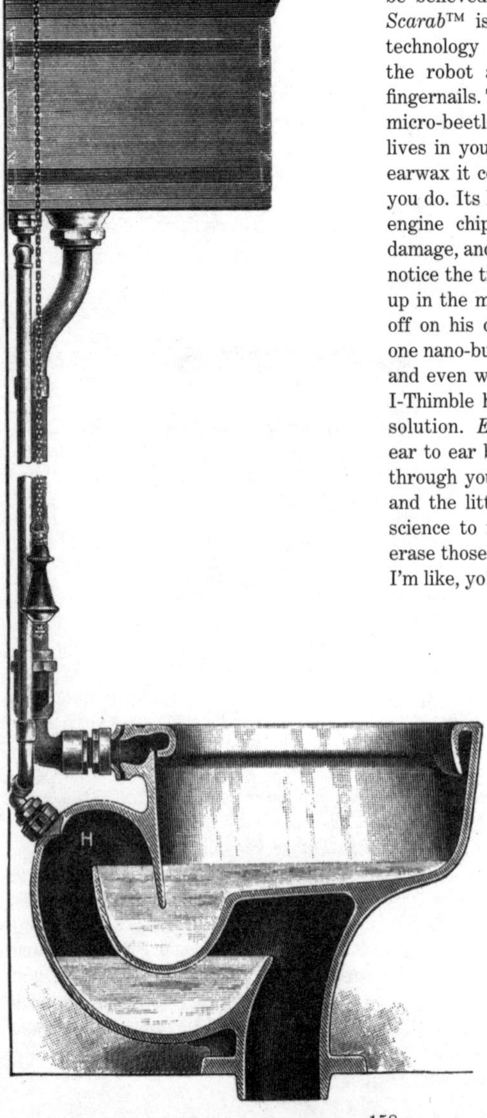

EARWAX SCARAB™—

is the most latest 'creation development experience' from Californian geeks with a factory—I-Thimble. And it's got to be believed to be experienced! *Earwax Scarab*™ is the chillinest use of nanotechnology since My Little Creature™, the robot ant that cleans under your fingernails. This eighteen carat gold ultra-micro-beetle (1.8mm when assembled) lives in your ear and is powered by the earwax it consumes, so it won't die until you do. Its long life Chronononoium 3™ engine chip is resistant to cotton bud damage, and after a while you really don't notice the tiny hum of the motor starting up in the morning, when the scarab sets off on his daily rounds. Trials involving one nano-bug in each ear caused dizziness and even wooziness in some subjects. So I-Thimble has come up with an inspired solution. *Earwax Scarab*™ gets from ear to ear by tunnelling a micro-passage through your brain. But you can't feel it and the little guy knows enough neuroscience to find the route least likely to erase those precious childhood memories. I'm like, yo! CrystalHearing™!

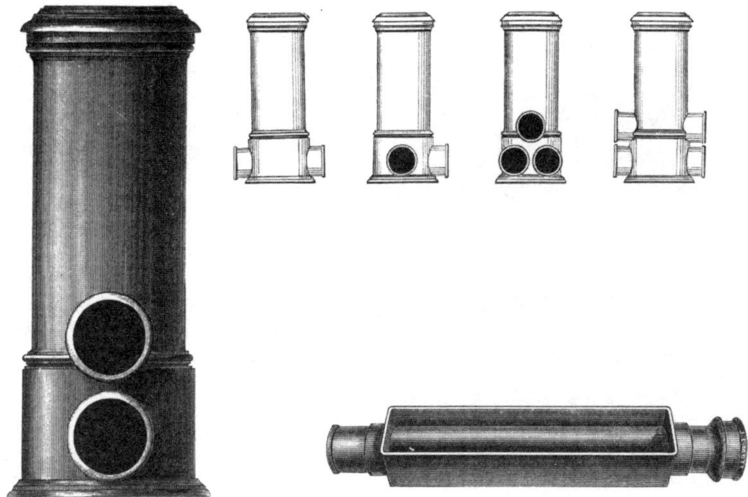

PBD ZZ9III—

Parcel Bomb Detectors Ltd have just brought out a glitzy new model and it's abso-Audrey Hepburn-lutely going to be the xpod for the late Naughties. The *PBD ZZ9iii* is fashioned from lightweight, organically brushed aluminium, so it looks and feels slinky and sexy. It is shaped like a miniature Labrador dog and bares the Semtex Rex logo ('the sniffer that snaffles the plotter') in electric blue—Zap! But just because it's machine-crafted, sleek and canine doesn't mean it can't pull its stats—it's able to detect a mivvi-sized package of C5 at eleven yards, which is like the equivalent of one as per thousand similes. This is edge of the razor stuff.

NEIGHBOUR WATCH HOODS—

are the newest and latest from Marsha McLuhan's Milan design labs: a must-have for those that must have. A bizarre and previously thought extinct form of radiation allows you to look right into your neighbours' living rooms and bedrooms. The hood itself uses extreme fibres made from plasticised lead, a saucy and magical compound that's handily like plastic in some ways and conveniently like lead in others. It attaches to the wall using Technigum™, is available in medium darkness or thick grey, and is surprisingly comfortable to wear once the goggles are calibrated. A low-key embarrassment alarm goes off (the factory setting appears to be the Gypsy Kings) if two *Neighbour Watch Hoods* are aligned accidentally on opposites sides of a wall. After all, it's no fun watching them watching you watching them etc—you might get caught in the rare but digitally documented 'voyeur vortex' (see below). Insurance is recommended.

ZEITGEIST III: SOUTH LONDON—

GameSphere™ ExoBod™ presents *Zeitgeist III: South London* for the Magnatrope Mombassa Console. This really is an ice cube for the cool gamers out there. It's much mo' better than *Zeitgeist II: West London*, because the controls are more responsive, the moves are more dynamic and the street edge has the edge. Using your joystick you have to identify the cultural artefacts that define contemporary ideologies, or define ideological culture in terms of identifying the contemporary —one or the other, it gets tricky after level 3. Excellent graphics throughout (the cognoscenti are particularly gruesome), though the conversation at some of the parties can be, like, vapid, and a couple of the car chases are way too credible. There's no doubt that it is a difficult game to play. In fact, unless you know the cheats, the manufacturers recommend psychoactive drugs for the top three levels. But you will undoubtedly keep wanting to come back for more. The rewards—should you get to level six, where you're finally just an immortal brain in a jar controlling a self-perpetuating and absurd monoculture from a triple-techno super-bunker on an isolated Pacific island—are wonderfully ephemeral and may cause seizures.

JOBSPEAK PALMWAFER™—

The *JobSpeak PalmWafer*™ is a real boon for those meetings when you find yourself sitting there thinking, 'what the hell does all this mean? I don't understand a word anyone's saying'. With an extraordinary 6G mote-memory, the *PalmWafer*™ not only feeds you 'the business lines that you need' on almost a dozen settings—from go-getting uber-corporation strategy meeting to disgruntled old shareholders in a hotel bar, from golf course putsch to organised crime caper run-through—but it will vibrate them into your palm and up your arm using a brand new technology that involves having fibre-optic cables installed in your arm. All you need to do if you want to speak the PalmWafer's suggestion—say, 'This shows what a fool I was to trust you! Middle management are gonna pay for this!'—is to open your mouth. Make sure to give it *your* voice sample. The default, for reasons unclear, is a ten-year-old girl from Weston-super-Mare.

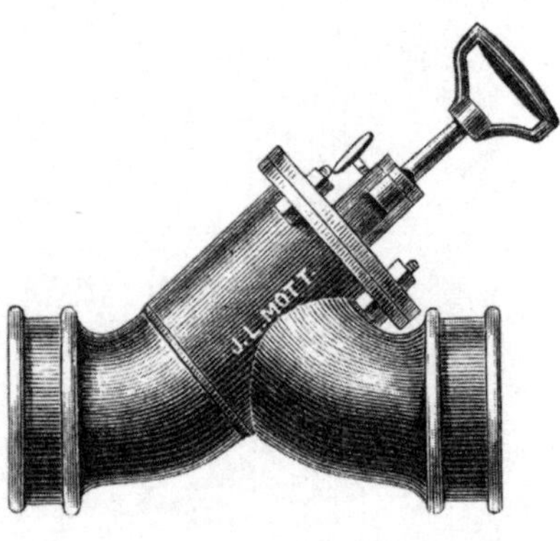

SELF-MEDIATION™ & OBJECTIFICATION DISCOVERY GIFT SET—

The perkiest of this job's perks is the old adagio—new gizmo, new experience. It certainly turned out to be true when for three months I house-tested the myriad micro-cams that are the *Self-Mediation™ & Objectification Discovery Gift Set.* The set, which runs twenty-fours hours a day and seven days a week, comprises six micro-cams in each room, so you can always get the best angle, plus four or five mobile cameras built into tiny robots that look and sound like bumblebees. These follow you around, or trail the cats, or just hover about in the garden to film any nature stuff that might happen while you're not there. They even come in the car with you. But they are fragile and you will need plenty of spares. In the first week, two of the bumblebee robot-cams filmed their own deaths—one at the paws of the cats, the other the victim of a real bumblebee attack while it was on flower-bed patrol. I felt bad, but both deaths made great TV and bee-cams are cheap.

The big question is whether the presence of all the cameras made my wife and I change our behaviour. The most notable changes were that my wife swore a lot less and I sat on the toilet at a radically different angle, so my good side was always on show. Another fairly reasonably sized question is how it felt to be the object of so much electronic mediation. Early on in particular, I enjoyed the attention and the way I looked on screen. But as the weeks rumbled along and rumours of my affairs and addictions started to spread, I tended to go from one room to another with a raincoat over my head, and I ended up getting aggressive with the bee-cams. I now regret this, though some of it was sort of watchable.

The other thing with the *Self Mediation™ & Objectification Discovery Gift Set* is that you spend more and more time watching what you did earlier until what you did earlier is watch what you did earlier than that (see above). And you film yourself doing this. So, not really for those with a sensitive stomach. Long-term? I'm definitely ready for my close-up.

PAUL BARKER *(Maidenhead)*

Drowning in stuff?

theenthusiast@theenthusiast.co.uk
THE ENTHUSIAST, PO BOX 239, BANGOR, BT20 5YB

* WISE WORDS * *

'THE GREAT SECRET OF MORALS IS LOVE;
OR A GOING OUT OF OUR OWN NATURE,
AND AN IDENTIFICATION OF OURSELVES WITH THE BEAUTIFUL
WHICH EXISTS IN THOUGHT,
ACTION, OR PERSON,
NOT OUR OWN.'

SHELLEY—(Defence of Poetry)

– WHAT I NEED –

I need a defining style.

GILLIAN BURT *(London)*

Up town top rankin'?

Still don't know what to listen to?

1. **FOUR TET: PAUSE** *(Domino Records)*. Fresh sounding electronic, yet organic, music from the UK.

2. **AUGUSTUS PABLO: KING TUBBYS MEET ROCKERS UPTOWN** *(Mango)*. Gritty and ethereal dub from the seventies.

3. **SHUGGIE OTIS: INSPIRATION INFORMATION** *(Luaka Bop)*. Sadly underrated soul record now happily re-released.

4. **HASSAN ERRAJI AND ARABESQUE: MARHABA** *(Riverboat Records)*. Warm Moroccan music with jazz inflections.

5. **ISSA BAGAYOGO: SYA** *(Six Degrees)*. There's plenty of extra-ordinary music coming out of Mali; this record offers something different.

6. **SIDESTEPPER: MORE GRIP** *(Palm Pictures)*. Vibrant salsa dance fusion from Colombia.

7. **TONY ALLEN: BLACK VOICES** *(Comet Records)*. Classic, tight, and modern afro-funk.

8. **ORANGE CAN: HOME BURNS** *(Regal)*. Dreamy, sixties-inspired indie from London.

9. **NEUROSIS: TIMES OF GRACE** *(Relapse)*. A furious blend of metal and pagan music. Approach with caution.

10. **BACHUE: THE BUTTERFLY** *(Big Bash Records)*. A stunning blend of modern and traditional Scottish folk.

11. **WIMME: GIERRAN** *(Northside)*. Incredible, heady mix of Sami chant and electronics.

12. **MURCOF: UTOPIA** *(Leaf)*. Unique. A stunning blend of orchestral and electronic minimalism from Mexico.

13. **THE CINEMATIC ORCHESTRA: EVERYDAY** *(Ninja Tune)*. What modern jazz is.

14. **BOOTY BREAKS VOL.2** *(Bootaay)*. Tight and gritty breaks geared for the clubs.

15. **TM JUKE: MAPS OF THE WILDERNESS** *(Tru Thoughts)*. Soulful and jazzy; gentle trip-hop.

16. **FUTURE WORLD FUNK 1/2/3** *(Ocho)*. Perfect demonstrations of how different musics can be put together.

17. **HUUN-HUUR TU AND THE BULGARIAN VOICES ANGELITE: FLY, FLY MY SADNESS** *(Jaro Medien)*. Extraordinary mix of Mongolian and Bulgarian vocals.

18. **NORDIC ROOTS NORTHSIDE SAMPLER 1/2/3** *(Northside)*. Perfect and inexpensive routes into Scandinavian folk.

19. **TALK TALK: SPIRIT OF EDEN** *(EMI)*. Essential and refreshing still.

20. **SUSUMU YOKOTA: GRINNING CAT** *(Leaf)*. Musical poetry. Just a small part of a rich Japanese electronic scene.

LEE MATTHEWS *(Orpington)*

You dancin'?

A YOUNGER READER WRITES

I have my Travel Happy Cup, my inflatable potty,
my yin yin blanket (which sometimes I wash
all by myself), and I'm ready to go.

A brisk wind ruffles the pampas grass.
My tongue runs dry. Travel tends to upset
my equilibrium. Sun shines on the pavement.

I put on my woolly hat—then take it off—
my one-piece snow-suit, my latest Clarks
and also some spare trousers, just in case.

A plastic bag—yes!—with *Spot the Dog*,
and my gloves connected by elastic.

I'm fed up with people wiping my arse.
I've played with all my toys.
I want to be one of the boys.

P. LENNARD *(Oxford)*

On the run?

theenthusiast@theenthusiast.co.uk

THE ENTHUSIAST, PO BOX 239, BANGOR, BT20 5YB

Recipes

THE FOLLOWING will make a good picnic on the beach at Whitstable, or in Bangor, or elsewhere.

ROMANY PIE

Serves 4–6

1 tender rabbit
1/2 lb beef steak
2 teaspoonsful chopped parsley
1/2 lb pork sausages
salt
pepper
nutmeg
stock

Soak rabbit in cold, salted water for one and a half hours. Wipe dry, and joint (rabbit). Skin sausages and with floured hands and make meat into round balls. Cut steak into small pieces. Arrange rabbit, sausage and beef in pie dish. Sprinkle over the parsley, grated nutmeg, pepper and salt to taste. Add stock, cover with pastry and bake slowly for one and half hours after the pastry has arisen.

BOEUF À LA PROVENÇALE

Serves 4–6

2 lb stewing beef
2 tablespoons vinegar
2 sticks celery cut into one-inch lengths
1 gill red wine
12 shallots
1 lb carrots cut into thin rings
2 cloves garlic
strips of bacon for larding
small bay leaf
4 oz fat bacon
salt
pepper

Renowned for your little impromptu meals?

theenthusiast@theenthusiast.co.uk

The Enthusiast, PO Box 239,
BANGOR BT20 5YB

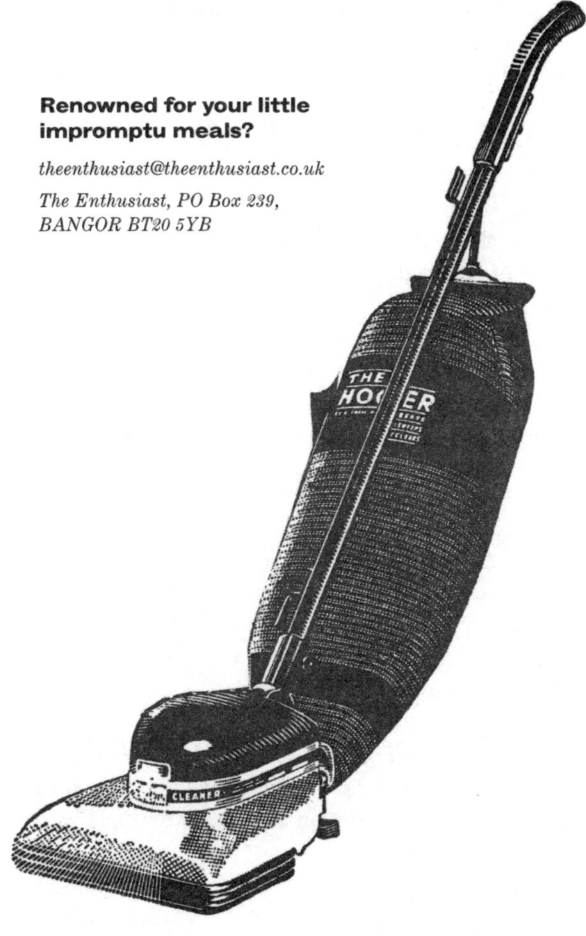

Cut the beef into cubes and lard each with a small strip of bacon. (To lard, make a cut in the cube and push a small bit of bacon in. Obviously.) Put into a deep dish with the wine, vinegar, and seasoning. Leave to marinade for 3 to 4 hours. Heat the 4 oz of fat bacon, finely chopped, and brown the onions, carrots, garlic and celery. Add the meat, and fry together for about five minutes. Add the marinade and 10 oz more of red wine, 8 oz more of bacon rinds well blanched and cut into small pieces, and a bouquet garnet. Cover the casserole dish tightly – really tightly – then allow to simmer on the hot plate for about four hours, or in a slow oven for about seven hours.

SWEET CAKE

4 eggs
flour equal in weight to the eggs
castor sugar equal to the weight of the flour
butter equal to the weight of the castor sugar
lemon peel grated

Mix sugar and flour with eggs, and cream the butter. Add the lemon peel with the butter and mix all well together. Put into a well-buttered cake tin and bake in a quick oven. The quicker the better. Quick as you like.

MANGEL-WURZEL WINE

1 gallon of mangels
1 gallon of water
3 lb sugar
1 oz yeast
1/2 oz hops

Clean the mangels by washing well and take off the roughest roots. Cut into dice and boil in the water one hour. Strain (this is important). Put the sugar in the liquid and stir until dissolved. Add the hops and when lukewarm – the water – sprinkle the yeast on top. Leave for three weeks to ferment. Strain and bottle. Drink.

CAROL COOPER *(Stafford)*

Picture the scene: a busy restaurant kitchen; flames dancing; 'chefs de parties' scurrying prettily hither and thither; a stained and apoplectic 'sous-chef' ranting drunkenly from atop the chest freezer...

... Kitchen Porters cowering under a barrage of sexual harassment and filthy pans; stunning waitresses curling their perfect lips, their pert bosoms quivering beneath too, too translucent blouses as the inadequates around them concuss themselves against fridges trying to gain a discreet eyeful.

A hush descends as Gaston, the redoubtable *mâitre d'hôtel*, Roquefort-breathed and many moustached, father of a hundred children and a thousand horrors, scourge of *sommelier* and critic alike, strides into the glow of the heat lamps. Thrusting an unfortunate *garçon* into the path of the thundering dessert trolley, he glowers at the assembled misfits and *parvenus* of kitchen life. 'Pigs!' he barks. 'The son of a syphilitic whore on table *onze* has chosen the *chateaubriand*.' A nearby *commis-chef* crosses himself in anticipation of the dreadful declaration Gaston's furious visage warns him is imminent. 'He wants it ...' Gaston pauses, glancing around the Mordorian abyss of the three-starred kitchen, ensuring that every eye is focused firmly upon him, and spitting vehemently into a nearby green salad, 'He wants it,' he roars, 'WELL DONE'.

A deafening chorus of phlegmatic snorting fills the vaulted, soot-besmirched hall as the chefs compete as to who can extract the deepest, greenest, most antediluvian mucilaginous *bonne bouche*. 'Give him the special sauce!' he hisses as the staff assemble around the meat station to 'dress' the offending cut.

Gaston strides forth on to the restaurant floor, his entourage of *garçons* and flunkies snorting and whooping behind him. Silence falls as he surveys the dining room, his minions peering between his legs and peeping from the folds of his voluminous trousers. Without diverting his gaze from table eleven, he reaches to his left; arresting a spoonful of soup mere millimetres from the lips of a petrified patron.

'And how is your meal?' he purrs. The diner opens his mouth to respond.

'Sir?' prompts Gaston. The benighted customer glances down at the calloused, adamantine talon delicately pinching his soup spoon. His eyes slowly travel up the immaculate black gabardine sleeve until, as they reach Gaston's improbable moustaches, the *mâitre d'hôtel* releases the spoon, spattering hot *bouillabaisse* across his victim's cheek. 'Excellent,' he growls as the whimpering wretch grabs for his napkin, 'I am delighted that everything meets with your approval.'

He steps quickly to the entrance from the lobby and refuses entry to the president's mistress. 'I will report this to my friends!' she spits, 'you will hear more of this!'

Gaston leans forward. '*Merci Madame*, you are too kind. Please do mention my name to *Monsieur le President*, and give him my very best wishes for his re-election campaign. It would be such a tragedy for our nation if it were to be derailed by ... untimely revelations, *n'est-ce pas*?'

Strolling away from the suddenly pale courtesan, Gaston finally reaches table *onze* at the same time as a charred and smouldering lump of carbonised flesh. As the patron recoils from the smouldering meat, Gaston murmurs from just behind his left ear '*Chateaubriand*.' The man jumps as Gaston continues, 'Well ... done.' Turning, the patron flinches at Gaston's steely gaze.

'D'you know?' he stammers, 'what I really want is, well, just a plain and simple hamburger. Would that be possible? Please?'

A slow, languid grin spreads across Gaston's pockmarked features. 'An excellent choice, *Monsieur L' Ambassadeur*. I will personally supervise the creation of your ... burger.'

With a click of his patent leather heels he wheels and glides towards the kitchen, leaving the sepulchral echoes of a low and guttural chuckle in his wake.

JOSH BROWN *(Brighton)*

Would madam like to see the dessert menu?

theenthusiast@theenthusiast.co.uk
THE ENTHUSIAST, PO BOX 239, BANGOR, BT20 5YB

LIVES OF THE FAMOUS

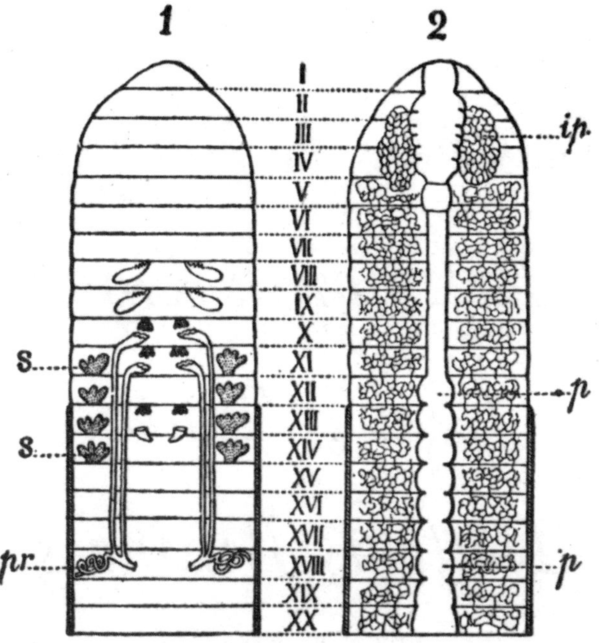

ALBRECHT DÜRER—Albrecht Dürer wasted three years of his life working on the Holy Roman Emperor Maximilian I's Triumphal Arch. The arch was made up of 192 separate parts and measured 10 feet wide by 11 feet high. Dürer was designer in chief: also employed on the project were an architect, an historian, and a company of craftsmen. The Arch features four Habsburg emperors on columns, Roman and German emperors on pedestals, 108 coats of arms, heralds and trumpeters on cornices, apes on steps, and goats on ledges. Under the cupola stands Maximilian in his coronation robes.

Unfortunately, Emperor Maximilian couldn't afford to have the Arch made up in stone or in marble: the project only ever existed as a woodcut on paper.

DOUGLAS GORE *(Knebworth)*

Good on paper?

theenthusiast@theenthusiast.co.uk THE ENTHUSIAST, PO BOX 239, BANGOR, BT20 5YB

Business is Religion.

Religion is God.

God is Truth.

Truth is Business.

ANDY WARD (*Swaffham*)

You're a lightweight. You're fired!

theenthusiast@theenthusiast.co.uk THE ENTHUSIAST, PO BOX 239, BANGOR, BT20 5YB

– HYMN –

34

AND THIS IS A PICTURE of me living,
Autumn came with wind and gold,
So I beat out the rhythm of an unfamiliar hymn
To make the people nervy and bold.

I told them it was their decision,
I said that God had made no plan,
That capital had and it was to our detriment
Severing further the capabilities of man.

And? And so I dipped my pen into the Thames Estuary.
It was cold. I had spent a night on the rocks,
Which surface sometimes as the sea sucks eastwards
Wrecked and lonely but for two books.

And I burnt one so I could read the other
And as morning came I did not regret my choice,
Brilliant and at once, bloody the length of it,
Thrown — imperious to human voice.

And so I stepped away, picked up my shoes and
stepped away,
Leaving a small pile of belongings on that deserted beach;
Not mine, somebody else's; my belongings I kept with me;
Bits mostly, beyond reach.

KEVIN NORMAN *(Botusfleming)*

Hallelujah?

theenthusiast@theenthusiast.co.uk

The Enthusiast, PO Box 239,
BANGOR BT20 5YB

ITCHY INTERNAL ORGANS

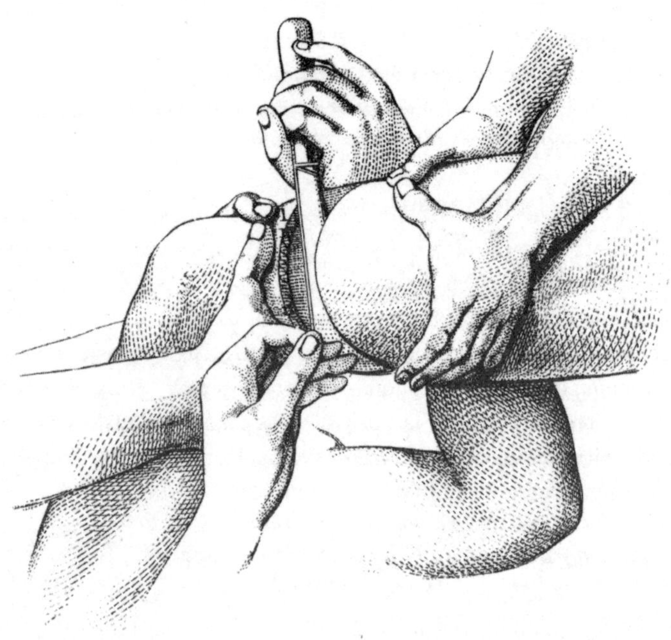

Though largely beneficent, Mother Nature is on occasion less than kind to her progeny. The first example of her sometime wilful bad intent that enters my brain is haemorrhoids (the thought of haemorrhoids entering the brain is, I confess not a little gruesome). Other examples are not hard to find. Despite her few parental failings, however, I submit that we all ought to club together and buy Mother Nature a big bunch of flowers. My reason is this : she has chosen not to bestow upon the human race the phenomenon of itchy internal organs.

Itchy internal organs! The very thought chills me to the core! What terror, what torment would be involved in having, say, an itchy spleen! Even as I write about it, I feel I should stop ; I am afflicted by a superstitious thought that my merely mentioning itchy spleens will summon that phenomenon from its slumber in the realm of the merely possible, and drag it into the dazzling and unpalatable light of the actual. How achingly unbearable that would be—an itch that

1. could not be scratched ; and
2. being no mere surface irritation, would have invaded the most private of spaces.

And imagine the procedure for ridding oneself of such an itch. There would simply be no alternative : it would be surgery or nothing. Picture the scene. You are admitted to hospital with an itchy pancreas. You are anaesthetised and wheeled to theatre, where you are surrounded by green-gowned medical staff. Lights flash and monitors beep on dizzyingly arcane hi-tech equipment. 'Scalpel!' a doctor orders. The instrument is passed to her, and she makes her cold incision with unconscious, practised ease. Her begloved hand enters the fresh-gaping hole, and finds the pancreas.

She scratches, and you are sewn up.

Hours later, you awake, your mind fogged with the anaesthetic. You purse your dry lips, and, with what seems a Herculean effort, you speak. 'Down a bit, and to the left,' you say.

PETER HERISSONE-KELLY *(Carnforth)*

Need a hand?

theenthusiast@theenthusiast.co.uk

THE ENTHUSIAST, PO BOX 239, BANGOR, BT20 5YB

A Ham Sandwich

TRY THIS. Go to your fridge and your cupboard (let's assume you have a fridge and a cupboard). Remove three items at random – tinned or fresh, it doesn't matter. The chances are they will all contain, or be sprayed with, or treated with, at least one of the following: acetic acid, aka **E260**; aspartame; phosphoric acid, aka **E338**; benzoic acid, aka **E210**; MSG, aka **E621**; something called Brown FK; and/or quinoline Yellow, aka **E104**.

Or try this. Make yourself a meal. Something easy. OK, so you haven't got the time or the necessary ingredients. A sandwich then, at least. Can you do a sandwich? Everyone can do a sandwich. Good. Go on. Any kind of sandwich. A ham sandwich, maybe. Obviously not if you're Jewish or Muslim. Have you done it? OK. Put it on a plate. Now, contemplate your sandwich. You know what's in it? Ham, and bread, right, and maybe some margarine and mayonnaise?

Wrong.

What you're got on your plate is water, salt, modified potato starch, dextrose, gelatine, carboxymethylcellulose, paprika extract, tri- and polyphosphates, sodium nitrate, potassium nitrate, sodium ascorbate, and spice extracts. And that's just the ham, 'Packaged In a Protective Atmosphere For Freshness', if you're lucky.

You ever think of converting?

What is all this shit? Do you know? Are you interested? You're eating it every day. Have you ever even thought about it? No, probably not. It's like everything else. No one thinks about anything until that Thing comes up and hits them in the face with a piece of 2" x 4".

I have been trying to explain this to my social worker and my psychiatrist: a ham sandwich is not merely ham and bread.

ANDY HODGSON *(Bath)*

Fatted calf?

theenthusiast@theenthusiast.co.uk

The Enthusiast, PO Box 239,
BANGOR BT20 5YB

Christmas

GAME PIE (LEICESTERSHIRE)

Serves 6–8

1 portion puff pastry
1 pheasant
4 oz bacon
1 hard-boiled egg
12 oz steak
1/2 pint stock
1 egg (not hard-boiled)
salt and pepper

Cut the pheasant into pieces and slice the meat, bacon and hard-boiled egg. Put all these into a pie dish in alternating layers and add the stock. Cover with pastry, brush with (the other) beaten egg and put first into a hot oven until the pastry lid has risen and then lower the oven temperature so that the meat can cook more slowly. Bake for about 1 hour. This pie can also be eaten cold, and is good for rather special picnics. Not suitable for microwaves.

HEATHER WINE (DARTMOOR)

heather (when it is in full bloom)
water – one gallon to 4lbs sugar
2 lemons
2 oranges
1oz yeast
a large slice of toast

1. Cut heather when in full bloom – making sure to remove every last trace of bracken – cover with water and boil for one hour. Then strain the liquid off and measure. Leave until lukewarm.

2. Slice the oranges and lemons into the liquid, add the sugar and stir well until it is dissolved. Spread the yeast onto both sides of the toast and float it (the toast) in the liquid. Leave 14 days to ferment, then skim and strain and bottle. Keep for 6 months. Disguise.

YULE BREAD (YORKSHIRE)

Put 1lb flour into a basin with a pinch of salt. Dissolve 1/2oz yeast in a cupful of warm water and stir into the flour. Let it stand for 1 hour in a warm place then add 1/2lb butter (creamed), 1/2lb sugar, half a grated nutmeg, 3/4lb currants, and pour into tins. Bake in a moderate (as opposed to an average) oven for about 2 hours. It is very nice buttered.

In the second week of December plant cob nuts and fruit trees. You can still plant fruit trees if the weather is open.

WENDY BETRAM *(Leopardstown)*

QUIZZES
& QUESTIONNAIRES

Twenty Questions

ONE

Yes?

TWO

No?

THREE

True or False?

[a] That certain facts are ignored is proof of their importance.
[b] Truth cannot be found by intellect alone.
[c] The children of the rich deserve better.
[d] It is possible to succeed and be right beyond one's intentions.

FOUR

Is this what you wanted to achieve?

FIVE

Show by definition that you are aware of the differences in meaning between the words in the following pairs:

> precept, percept; eccentric, egocentric; indict, indite; geography, topography; muscadine, muscadin; paraphrase, periphrasis; subsidence, subsistence; tatting, crotcheting; enfilade fire, defilade fire; salvo, barrage; pastiche, pasquinade; plankton, amoeba.

SIX

Name and illustrate any four rhetorical devices.

SEVEN

Is this what you wanted to achieve?

EIGHT

Are you fully conscious of:

[a] the unalterable laws of the universe?
[b] your complete isolation in time?
[c] the inevitability of doom?

NINE

Give in your own words the meaning of the following words and phrases:

> smiling intelligent detachment; high comedy; integral; stunning; crampon; osmotic pressure; alpha particle; Tolpuddle Martyrs; realism; suspended animation; premonitory moistening; barbarous ejaculations; fluctuant; hard currency; invisible exports; the Indian rope trick; quadratic equation; Cartesian doubt; the categorical imperative; the golden mean; toad-in-the-hole; derivative; anachronistic; inchoate; angst; derivative art; cheap money; nuclear fission.

TEN

Where do we go from here?

ELEVEN

Wherein lies happiness?

TWELVE

Write short definitions of the following words to show that you understand their meaning:

> picaresque; theosophy; estaminet; protoplasm; obbligato; phlebitis; theodolite; vortex; saxifrage; anacoluthon; sauerkraut; uvula; shillelagh; casein; asymptote; aposiopesis; virginals.

THIRTEEN

Give the English equivalent of these phrases:

> ab ovo; pons asinorum; agent provocateur; Deo volonte; ecce signum; sine qua non; faux pas; al fresco; Fata Morgana; fracas; feuilleton; enfant perdu; ruse de guerre; hors de combat; prie-Dieu; canaille; de trop; rara avis.

FOURTEEN

The following sentences are in jumbled order. Rearrange them into their proper order.

> What is it that makes a man strong, stronger than the whole world? What is it that makes a man great, admired by his fellow creatures, well pleasing in God's sight? What is it that makes a man unshakeable, more unshakeable than the rock? What is it that makes him weak, weaker than a child? What is it that makes him soft, softer than wax?
> It is love.

FIFTEEN

Write an essay on one of the following:

[a] *The Oxford English Dictionary*
[b] War
[c] Death
[d] Famine
[e] *The Rights of Man.*
[f] The duties of man.
[g] The Bible
[h] *Das Kapital* (Karl Marx)
[i] *The Prince* (Machiavelli)
[j] The excess sugar of a diabetic culture rotting the nerve of life and literature
[k] Pavlov's Dogs
[l] The Ivory Tower
[m] *The Wealth of Nations*
[n] The Survival of the Fittest
[o] As for Paul, he made havoc of the Church

SIXTEEN

Give equivalents in modern English for the following:

> rheum; billet-doux; brimstone; buss; alchemy; the king's-evil; betimes; turnkey; motley; warlock; stithy; cony-catcher; yare; eek; tapster; yclept; avaunt; maugre.

SEVENTEEN

Without sacrificing the basic meaning rewrite the following passages in your own words and in as lucid and simple a manner as possible:

> The One remains, the many change and pass;
> Heaven's light forever shines, Earth's shadows fly;
> Life, like a dome of many-coloured glass,
> Stains the white radiance of Eternity,
> Until Death tramples it to fragments.

> inque brevi spatio mutantur saecla animantum
> Et quasi cursores vitai lampada tradunt

But, first, whom shall we send
In search of this new World?
    whom shall we find
Sufficient? who shall tempt with
    wandering feet
The dark, unbottomed, infinite Abyss,
And through the palpable obscure
    find out
His uncouth way, or spread his
    aery flight,
Upborne with indefatigable wings
Over the vast Abrupt, ere he arrive
The happy Isle?

EIGHTEEN

What does the Bible say about the following:

[a] The love of money.
[b] The price of wisdom.
[c] The foolishness of God.
[d] The wise.
[e] A righteous man.
[f] God's ears.
[g] The eyes of the blind.

NINETEEN

Name ten emotions.

TWENTY

Feel them.

• *Credit will be given for clear working*

Fig. 1

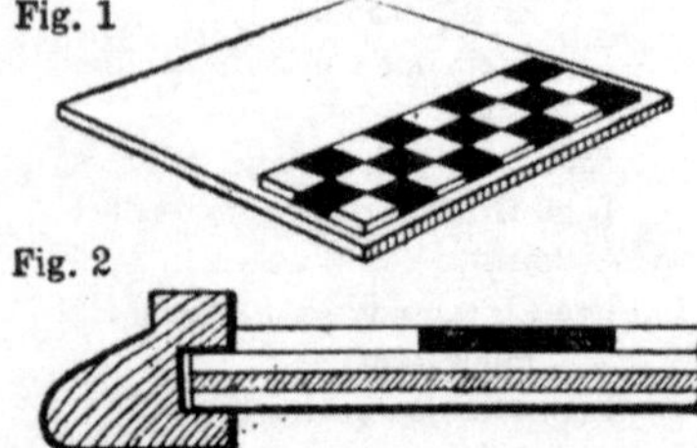

Fig. 2

Twenty Answers

1 Yes.

2 No.

3 Every day.

4 A tin of mixed biscuits.

5 With a pencil.

6 Blue.

7 Can insufficiencies in a pastry be compensated for by the quantity of the meat?

8 In Sanskrit aesthetics there are said to be 9 feelings that art can excite: wonder, joy, sexual pleasure, pity, anguish, anger, terror, disgust, laughter.

9 A small circle is as infinite as a large circle.

10 Sorry.

11 What's not to fear?

12 Sir Thomas Malory.

13 The contemplation of a neatly folded ham sandwich.

14 Norfolk.

15 Peckham.

16 Auden.

17 In bed.

18 Occasionally.

19 Sometimes.

20 Never.

theenthusiast@theenthusiast.co.uk
THE ENTHUSIAST, PO BOX 239, BANGOR, BT20 5YB

QUIZZES
& QUESTIONNAIRES

How equable are you*?*

Feeling middling? Moderate? Unusually mild? You could be succumbing to the latest fad that's swooping the nation and unlog-jamming a slewerage of emotional responses that can fairly be described as temperate. Of course, only doctors and other passport-signers are really lofty enough to get any kind of hardcore 'I am the kestrel of objectivity'-style low-down on the crazy swooshes and under-eddies that raddle our sparkly lives. But that doesn't stop us coming up with a questionnaire to let *you*, the person reading *this*, know your equability quotionale on a scale of 1–17.

Get a Uniball 0.8 mm fineline roller-ball in black, pull up a cosey and tick the boxes. It could (assuming a universe of infinite possibility) save your life.

ONE

A friend asks you to help him (or her) prepare for an open-ended ♠ 'War on Terror'. ♥♥♥♥♥♥♥♥♥♥♥♥♥♥

Do you?

a [ ] Politely say that you don't think jihad is for you.
b [ ] Advise him (or her) not to plan, but to improvise.
c [ ] Suggest that a nice cup of tea is as good a way as any to start planning for a long-term, low-level, dirty war.

TWO

A street crazy insists ♣ that German engineering ♣ is overrated.

Do you?

a [ ] Lend him a recent *Which?* guide.
b [ ] Pull his whiskers and tell him what a rascal he is.
c [ ] Retort that any species with stereoscopic vision and a functioning cerebellum can see that your Audi A3 in triple matt black with extra black, light-absorbent, nano-fibre interior stomps all over his Asda trolley.

THREE

You're at home watching *EastEnders.* ♠

Do you?

a [ ] Shoot up.
b [ ] Shoot the TV.
c [ ] Shoot yourself.

FOUR

After *EastEnders* ♠ there is a documentary about ♥♥ what would happen ♣♣ if the earth was hit by an asteroid with a dinosaur riding on it.

Do you?

a [ ] Wish that you could watch it, but the TV is now smouldering, bullet-riddled wreckage.
b [ ] Realise that you've missed the documentary because you've

been staring at the wall for an hour. Then discover a pool of drool on your chest.

c [ ] Think you could probably reach the phone to call an ambulance, but you can't move your arm. And it dawns on you how much blood you're losing.

FIVE

You come home to find that your seven-year-old son is watching ♥♥♥♥ a raunchy ♣ Christina Aguilera ♣ video.

Do you?

a [ ] Make him wash his eyes out with carbolic and promise never to watch BBC *News 24* again.
b [ ] Slump down on the sofa and say, 'This is okay. But the Dirrty video. Man, you could almost taste it.'
c [ ] Get out the Jimi Hendrix. It should still work.

SIX

Some people knock ♣♣ on your door and start talking about ♣♣♠♥♣ ♠♥ ♣ ♣ ♠♥♠♥♣♥♣♣♠♥♠♥♠ God. ♥

Do you?

a [ ] Suggest that they come in – you're about to watch the widescreen version of *Woodstock*.
b [ ] Tell yourself not to worry. Things probably won't get ugly. But if they do, you've always got that .38 tucked in the back of your jeans.
c [ ] Gibber like a baboonatic until they withdraw, befuddled.

SEVEN

A former friend who has ♠ now gone fully bananas ♠ invites you to a talk he's giving at the local youth club, entitled ♦♦ 'Jesus, Aliens and Freemasonry – the Facts'. ♦♦

Do you?

a [ ] Decide to go in case there's a bar.
b [ ] Fire-bomb the youth club – the fool's gonna tell them everything.
c [ ] Send the invitation back with 'YOU'RE NEXT' scribbled on it in blood.

EIGHT

A global conspiracy involving ♦♦ Jesus, Aliens and Freemasonry ♦♦ has taken over the future.

Do you?

a [ ] Just go in to work as normal. It's not like they're going to want to wreck the economy or anything.
b [ ] Hide out in the woods.
c [ ] Wish you'd gone to the damned meeting.

NINE

Your local paper is running a competition to discover some trivial nonsense.

Do you?

a [ ] Visit the local library to do a spot of research.
b [ ] Visit Antibes.
c [ ] Visit a terrible vengeance on them all.

TEN

You are at a Ferrero Rocher party ♥♥♥♥♥♥♥♥♥♥ The ambassador approaches you and discreetly suggests that you adjourn to an anteroom for informal talks with the French envoy about a joint EU policy on Iraq.

Do you?

a [ ] Shrug and say, 'What's Iraq?'
b [ ] Shout, 'Goddamit it, chocolate boy, I've got men on the ground down there!'
c [ ] Say, 'Oh Monsieur Ambassador ... Are you familiar with 'Ace of Spades' by Motorhead?'

ELEVEN

The babysitter arrives wearing a barely concealed explosive belt. You don't wish to appear rude, ♦♣♠♥♦ but feel you should voice your suspicion that she is a suicide bomber.

Do you?

a [ ] Greet her with a smile and say, 'Shall I take your coat and your explosive belt?'
b [ ] Try to snip the wires while she is making herself a snowball.
c [ ] Say, 'Can I press it? I've never pressed one before. Can I?'

TWELVE

You have reached a point in your life where you can no longer distinguish between ♥♥ tragedy and comedy. ♥♥

Do you?

a [ ] Change your name to Webster.
b [ ] Call home for reassurance.
c [ ] Watch more *Trisha.* She seems to understand.

....

Well, that's it – all the information needed to computise your personal equability quotionale. You'll be amazed at just what a lot of stuff is revealed by analysing that quotidian existence of yours.

The scoring is easy. [a] is one point, [b] is two, [c] is three – for the first four questions. Thereafter, [a] is worth two points for the next five questions (after which it alternates between four and three) as long as you score no more than three [c]s over the next five questions. [b] is always worth two points (except for questions 7 and 9 where it is worth nothing) and [c] is usually worth three points (as long as you score fewer than five [b]s) except on questions 7, 8 and 10, where it is worth one point.

HOW DID YOU DO?

If your score is less than fifteen points (Quotionale 9), you are as mild as a May morn. You're mellow and fruity or something (Emily's handwriting).

If your score is more than fifteen but less than twenty-seven (Quotionale 14), you enjoy being at one with your people, but you are capable of dividing and ruling with cold efficiency.

If your score is more than twenty-seven points (Quotionale 17) – ain't no more to add, you bad.

Take it easy now.

theenthusiast@theenthusiast.co.uk
THE ENTHUSIAST, PO BOX 239, BANGOR, BT20 5YB

QUIZZES
& QUESTIONNAIRES

Distinctions and definitions

ONE

PLEASE DISTINGUISH BETWEEN THE FOLLOWING:

1. a. HIGHWAYMAN and b. PIRATE.
2. a. AUDIENCE and b. SPECTATORS.
3. a. SPADE and b. SHOVEL.
4. a. MONOLOGUE and b. DUOLOGUE.
5. a. VEIN and b. ARTERY.
6. a. CUPID and b. EROS.
7. a. ROMAN NOSE and b. GRECIAN NOSE.
8. a. FLOTSAM and b. JETSAM.
9. a. ARCADIAN and b. ORCADIAN.
10. a. DRIFTER and b. TRAWLER.

TWO

RIGHT OR WRONG?

1. The wise men followed an angel.
2. Reading was once a pleasure, but is now a painful necessity.
3. Moses was lame.
4. Zion was called the Holy Hill.
5. Blessed are the meek: for they shall see God.
6. A tong is half a pair of tongs.
7. The boiling point of water is always the same.
8. Many rivers cannot quench love.
9. God tempers the wind to the shorn lamb.
10. The moon is older than the earth.

THREE

WHAT IS THE MEANING OF THE FOLLOWING WORDS?

1. vivats
2. gabelle
3. leman
4. drunter und drüber

5. sub rosa
6. lapsus linguae
7. Aubusson
8. finis coronat opus
9. cambric
10. o peior porco come a melhor glande

FOUR

PICK OUT A SMALL ERROR OF STATEMENT IN YOUR COPY OF *THE ENTHUSIAST ALMANACK.*

FIVE

WRITE A SHORT ESSAY ON ONE OR MORE OF THE FOLLOWING.

1. Sinn Féin
2. Europe
3. The Book of Kells
4. Mazes
5. Sailing to Byzantium
6. Pandering
7. Arresting Metaphors
8. The Dead Sea Scrolls
9. The Signs of the Zodiac
10. Chimpanzees

SIX

WHICH OF THE FOLLOWING ARE ARTISTS AND WHICH ARE CHEESES? WHICH ARE BOTH?

1. Cellini
2. Giorgione
3. Gorgonzola
4. Parmigiano
5. Reggiano
6. Wensleydale
7. Epoisses
8. Spenlow
9. Jorkin
10. Jarlsberg

Brainteaser?

theenthusiast@theenthusiast.co.uk
THE ENTHUSIAST, PO BOX 239, BANGOR, BT20 5YB

QUIZZES
& QUESTIONNAIRES

No, Really, How Are *You?*

Let's go the extra furlong and find out how you are – no, really, how are you? This questionnaire for quizlings lets you score yourself silly – why not use the back of an envelope and that lovely fat carpentry pencil that's been sitting in the box all these decades?

(NB. The scoring involves long division, so think about your answers. You might come out at 1.084 when you should really be a 2.175. Then the whole thing would be pointless.)

Here come the questions now. Ready?

ONE

The new job isn't turning out like you hoped.

Which statement best nails your brain feeling?

a [ ] Charlie, it was you.
b [ ] But Professor, dinosaurs have been extinct for millions of years.
c [ ] Darling, I'm tired.

TWO

You have been quoted on *Quote Unquote.*

Do you?

a [ ] Kill yourself.
b [ ] Do nothing – dead already.
c [ ] Take the job on the supertanker. You, a canvas holdall, the world.

THREE

You find out that the War on Terror started as a typo on a document originating from Uxbridge Magistrates Court. Apparently it should have read 'warrant error'. Numerate your emotional response.

a [ ] 5.
b [ ] 7.
c [ ] 9.

FOUR

Someone asks you how it all came to this.

Is this your response?

a [ ] Declarative.
b [ ] Interrogative.
c [ ] Imperative.

FIVE

You see a young person driving a Hillman Imp.

a [ ] Good.
b [ ] Bad.
c [ ] Indeed.

SIX

The lowest common denominator is secretly your favourite.

a [ ] You get what you deserve.
b [ ] You got what you reserved.
c [ ] Bugatti wood preserve.

SEVEN

You are given the Keys to the City.

Do you?

a [ ] Bite them. You need to know it's the real deal this time.
b [ ] Put them on the tag marked 'Garage & Shed'.
c [ ] Wake up. They're laughing at you.

EIGHT

Children seem to sense that you are not to be taken seriously.

Which strand of your narrative will you yoink?

a [ ] Avoid all youngsters, including your own.
b [ ] Embarrass the under-sevens with offers of alcohol and cigarettes.
c [ ] Take them fishing. They'll come round.

NINE

A door-stepping journalist is trying to get you to do some word-association.

Which answer comes closest to your possible response when she says, 'Frustration'?

a [ ] Radio 4.
b [ ] The sniper in the farmhouse just below the tree line.
c [ ] That game with the dice in a plastic bubble.

TEN

A taxi-driver claims he had that Noam Chomsky in the back of his cab.

What does he claim Chomsky talked about?

a [ ] Deep structure and universal grammar.
b [ ] Wayne Rooney.
c [ ] Media hegemony and the manufacture of consent.

ELEVEN

A subtle piece of authorial legerdemain sees you five thousand pounds richer.

What ya gonna do?

a [ ] Take it down the track, my son.
b [ ] Build a hotel on Park Lane.
c [ ] Give it to the poor. Lord knows they need it.

TWELVE

Polonius asks you what you are reading. You say:

a [ ] *Heat.*
b [ ] *The Koran.*
c [ ] *Addicted* by Tony Adams.

THIRTEEN

Your colleagues confess they don't share your sartorial style.

Do you?

a [ ] Take off the poncho.
b [ ] Get off the donkey.
c [ ] Lay down your pistols.

FOURTEEN

A genuine witch doctor from rural Zambia comes to stay with you. He presents some unique challenges. You might:

a [ ] Take him to the Royal Opera House.
b [ ] Take him to Lincoln Cathedral.
c [ ] Let him watch TV and go to a couple of Fulham home games. That's what he wants.

FIFTEEN

The new job just gets worse.

Which statement outlines your window?

a [ ] For God's sake, Professor! Shoot it! Shoot it!
b [ ] I agree with all the proposals in the quarterly report.
c [ ] The round window.

SIXTEEN

You're given the once-in-a-lifetime opportunity of attending the Smash Hits Poll Winners Party!

Who would you choose as your Hot Date?

a [ ] Ingres Hippard.
b [ ] Vortig Zune.
c [ ] Feltham Urqhart.

SEVENTEEN

You and some friends go for a game of football in the park, only to find that the government have moved the goalposts.

Do any of the following overlay your pattern?

a [ ] I shall send a note to Sir Richard.
b [ ] Jumpers it is.
c [ ] Ingres Hippard did this.

EIGHTEEN

Because of Fate your house has been repossessed. You take it like a person and then:

a [ ] Live at the warehouse. It's not the first time.
b [ ] Get involved with a commune on the Circle Line.
c [ ] Move in with that drunken poetess.

NINETEEN

A stranger rings and asks you if you've won a competition. You say:

a [ ] I'm so pleased for him. He always seemed so nice.
b [ ] That lousy rat! I shoulda fixed him when I had the chance.
c [ ] I hear the voices of the lost generations. They are voices of sorrow.

TWENTY

You, Jonathan Richman and the Modern Lovers are all at a car-boot sale.

But who wants what?

a [ ] The porcelain shire horse.
b [ ] The Edgar Wallace paperbacks.
c [ ] The replica firearm.

Jot up your points. It's 1.987 points for a right answer, 3.851 for a wrong, 2.539 for both. Now divide your total by 29.649.

Anything lower than 1.683 points, you're okay.

1.684 to 2.023 points, you're alright.

2.024 to 2.360 points, you're getting along.

2.361 points and above, you're fine. At least you know now.

QUESTIONNAIRES, QUIZZES AND COMPETITIONS compiled by
PAUL BARKER *(Maidenhead)*,
JONATHAN MACMILLEN *(Binsey)*,
VERONICA RULE *(Smerwick)*,
REVD. F. S. FRERE *(Braintree)*

theenthusiast@theenthusiast.co.uk
THE ENTHUSIAST, PO BOX 239, BANGOR, BT20 5YB

ANNOUNCEMENTS & ADVERTISEMENTS

FOR SALE

PERSONALISED BLURRY NUMBER PLATES. As seen on TV. Call Hepsibar 00565656

SELF-RAISING FLOWERS. £5 per gill. Call Mossery 1212 34567

DARK BULBS. £12 per caddy. Call Eddie 0700 BULBOUS

BLIGHTY WOUND. Offers. Call Wiffle.

EX-POLICE SLOTH TRAPS. Mats included. £50 each. Call Tove 677688585

CULTURAL RE-EVALUATION, full history. £29.99. Call Jess TVC15

OAK-AGED ACORNS. £8 for 20. Call Phil the Library 03299999

EXACTLY! Tel. 400300200

SKIP HIRE, Quaver rental, Wotsit disposal. DOA. Call Abdi 08000800

PRAVDA HANDBAGS. The real thing. Call Gerby 055 987651

POWDERED ELECTRICITY. Jazzing required. £15 per bushel. Tel Helen Highwater 077844478

SHOULDER PADS of giants. £150 pp. Call Davie 07777777

CART OF DARKNESS, some ambiguity on spindles, hence £73. Call 08796888

COY CARP. Shhhh. Call 011011001

ASBO framing, from £5. Call PD 07899999

DRIVEL. £17.50. Piffle £12.98. Call 0800444444

HAGGIS TWEED SUITS. Small-medium to medium-small. Call the number you first thought of.

JELLIED WHEELS, recently upgraded. £50. Call Miji 03663397

GENUINE NEW GUINEA PIGS from New Guinea—3 guineas each. Call 0700 NGGP

VOICES telling you to do stuff. You know the number.

TWO CORBIES, sold as pair only, sentimental reason. Call Brillo 089766666

PAPAL BULLS, Holy Cows. £280 each, buyer to collect. Call Geri 00000666

GLASS PASTE. Never opened. £30. Call Mr P. 0123456789

HOT AIR BABOON. At the top of his game. A bargain at £80. Call Wendy 08976888

TWO TICKETS for Abu Ghraib The Musical, third row of the stalls—£40 each. Call Maz 09898777

WISHES, Three—£4 or £2.50 each. Doh! Just rub the lamp

LARGE MAHAL. Must be scene. £650. Call Jello 03003444

INTIMATIONS OF IMMORTALITY, used once only, beautiful condition. £18. Call Bill 07000700

DRAGON DROPS. *£2.50 per quarter. Call Zog 007007800*

SECURITY CHIMERAS, organic camouflage as standard. Call Griff 09080765

NO BANANAS. Tel 7786004

FULL SET OF JE NE SAIS QUOITS. Boxed. Omnipresent @whimsicalnephew.co.aa

LIFETIME GUARANTEE, needs attention, only £40. Call Ja McCaroon

OLDEN DAYS, as new. £79.99. Tel Graham 0434303 22

BIG ISSUE, mister?

YOUTH's ignorance of its own qualities. £10? £12? Whatever

POTTERS BAR, some marks on veneer. £300. Two minor, semi-picturesque Cambridgeshire villages also available. Offers. Call Offa 013579 8642

LEOPARD-SKIN TIGER, beautiful piece of work, provenance etc. £15. Call Pfaff 000223444

TANTRIC YOGHURT: chi, ambivalence, fruits of the forest. £8 per stance. Tel Po 012034056

PENELOPE WILTON DIPTYCH. Genuine reason for sale. £270 ovno. Call Rich 0445732

GUTTERSNIPES, rags included, in need of some grubbing-up. Call Twenke 000700747

DODECAHEDRONS. £3. Call Bach 0111110

AXES OF EVIL, free to a good home (Axels of Evil also available). Call Moira

MIDAS TOUCH, rechargeable batteries included, £35. Call Fingers 0800443322

THUNDEROUS APPLAUSE, £7. Call Ian Crowd

BIRMINGHAM ACCENTS, West Midlands and Alabama, £10 or £15 the pair. Call Broyn 0990 232323

SECOND-HAND CHILDREN'S TOYS AND GAMES—including Corpse Mutilator, Spine Remover, Viscera 2, Brain Liquidiser, Cabbage Patch Apocalypse, Cindy. POA. Call Fleance 09902222

M25, sold as seen, buyer to collect, £400,000. Call Gerry 09904657

UNNATURALLY LARGE TENCH, one of a kind, genuine reason for sale, £250. Call Slim 09903467

ARTILLERY BARRAGE, London and South East only, call with coordinates, £500 ono. Call Sonia 099045321

FUMES, sale or swap, call with list. Call 099019874

BUNGEE WALKING, £15 per half hour. Call Leon C 099022289

BOURGEOIS RETICENCE, genuine 60s model, one lady owner, original racing green, first to see will buy, £650. Call Johnny, 09908456

CHARTISM, £18. Call Ida Spare 099063452

BURGLARY VIDEOS, no longer needed, boxed set of eight, including two massive houses in Notting Hill and a basement flat in Westbourne Park where there was f***ing gear everywhere. Neil done most of the damage. Call 09878888

TERROR PINS, £5 per bundle. Call Joy 0990 77777

1970s And 80s Board Games—Oil Crisis, Desert Hostage Dash, Grunwick Gorilla, Picket!, Re-unite the Nation, Tripoli Raider. POA. Call 0990254378

AFFABLE APE, £250. Call Amos 099086300

BOOTY LIQUORICE, £2 per bag. Call Traumara, 099055337

DERRIDA 3000LX, omnidisciplinary, universal fallacy adaptor, boxed as new, £420 ono. Call 099034765

TELLING REJOINDERS, £10 for three. Call Simone 099078091

METAPHYSICAL POTTERY, tea sets and mugs, from £5. Call Marve 099023648

PRE-WAR CERTAINTIES, £5 for twelve. Call 099095634

SITCOM LODGER, £18. Call Tel 0990

CHARLES BUKOWSKI-STYLE GREETING CARDS, £12 for 20, assorted designs and messages—including 'Do you f*** like your sister?', 'Gimme Bourbon' and 'No message, I'm unconscious'. Call Bunny 099014386

REPLACING ALL YOUR OLD TAPEWORMS WITH DIGITAL? Cheapest prices in the South Northern Area. Tel 0990387540

TWERPS, £70 for five. Call 0990376498

SOLAR EELS, £15 per pair. Call 099036453

MEANWHILE, £65. Call Paul 099015379

NOTHING SAYS 'I LOVE YOU' like a skateboarding Armadillo. Mother's Day, Valentine's, all occasions, £70. Call 099054758

BEEF WELLINGTON BOOTS, £30 per pair. Call Ian Neon 099099340

UMBRAGE TAKING. £50 per day. Call Harry (H.R.H.) 0207 435 7696.

VELVET SHOWER CURTAIN, royal blue, £70 ovno. Call Elvira 0208 5332506.

ORIGINAL 1950S ESTEEM MAGNIFIER, some damage to harness, will accept £150. gloomiseternal@hotmail.com

VARIOUS BACTERIA. Over 18s only. POA. Call Magnus 01392 263081.

UNICORN, low mileage, partial service history. £500 for quick sale. Call Sancho 0207 2091101.

PROMINENT VICTORIAN ENGINEERS. £80 each, 4 for £200. Call Izzie 0800 243407.

FIRE-DAMAGED PAPERBOYS. £20 per dozen. Call Ivan 01227 779082.

ISLE OF MAN, one lady owner, £475. Call Doug 01227 779082.

GENIUS PANTS, 34" waist, charcoal grey, hardly used. £25. Call Ling 0207 7420 9881.

CULT STATUS, £150. Call Sancho, as above.

INDUSTRIAL DENTAL FLOSS, £100 per tonne. Call Fingers 0207 431 4391.

GOOD HOME NEEDED FOR TOILET DUCKLINGS. Offers? Call Margaret (914) 395 2371.

LUNGFISH TRAINER. £25 p.h. 0207 7704 0474.

PUBERTY, £12. nobody@hotmail.com

DIGITAL WASHING MACHINE. Some pixels faulty on pre-wash. $40. 1-800-225-3998.

DECOROUS DOG. £18. 0207 465 0034.

MINIATURE EMPIRES (Rome, Spain, Mongol). £40 the set. 0207 727 8993.

MESOPOTAMIAN DEATH MASKS. Unwanted gift. £25 each. 0207 891 4567.

GAUCHO ACCESSORIES. Call Neil 0207 704 9776.

SECOND-HAND INSULTS. £2 for 10. Call 01279 623623.

NUCLEAR DETERRENT. Used once. £350 ovno. Call Nikolai 0207 316 9000.

FEELING LISTLESS, DEPRESSED AND ANXIOUS? Can't see a reason to go on? Pull yourself together, man! Institute of English Psychiatry. Call Carl 01202 440840.

KUNG FU VAMPIRE GHOST. Reliable runner. £80. Call Monkey 0208 433 3716.

MORAL CONSCIENCE. Hardly used. Write to: Mr President, White House, U.S.A.

LUXURY WATER. Offers. 0207 3874499.

FAULTY LIBIDO. Needs attention, hence £8. Call 0207 439 5000.

ELTON JOHN. Slightly soiled. Offers? Call Bernie 01733 898100.

INFLATABLE BUTTOCKS, J-Lo style. Need cleaning. 0207 917 3912.

TRILBY COUNSELLING. Rates negotiable. call Iggy. 001 319 335 2000.

THE DIARY OF A MOLE AGED 13½, large print. £9. Call Bruce 0987456456

BONE IDOL, reclining, scratches. £70. Call Tim on 01267 112211

SADISTIC ANIMAL PORN, if you've read this far you need immediate psychological help. Call the counselling hotline in confidence 0865 999999. Calls cost £5 per min. Your call may be recorded for training purposes.

SNAKES, ALIVE. Great Snakes. £6 per inch. Individually wrapped. Perfect Gift. 012345 ask for Sid.

AUTUMN LEAVES? And this time it's for good. Call the Child Support Agency 08457 133 133

MOUSE DEFLECTOR. £10.50 ovno. T. C. Thomas, 03330324

AURA OF POWER. £30. Tel. Craig, 03394421

PYRAMUS FRISBEES. Puck-o-matic. £5. Call Grandee 02284223

GILDED CHUBB. Buyer to collect. £18. Tel. B. Goldwater

TOP TRUMPS—Librarians, Junior Ministers, Regional Civil Servants. £3 per set. Department of Comics. 02364 6681

SEEING NO EVIL? Call J F for list. 0665667

NEW LEAVES. £6.50 for 2lb bag. Mulch also available—call for details. Bill W. 0338433

FUGS. £35. Tel. Tina T 09982467

BEEP THE BABY TO SLEEP—MOBILE PHONE MOBILE. £30 Call Vera Quietly. 03994157

ANTE UPPING. With Crucial Stage Recognition. Call Trent Raj. 0870 NO

TENDENCIES. Fifteen for £55.55. Ask for Doddy, 0769882

LIMITLESS RICHES. Send sae and £10 to Box 24 inside Box 9.

HIP-O-MATIC SELF-SURGERY APPLICATOR. £100. Call Maureen 0444831

VIRTUAL CRISIS TENT. Wan lady owner. £80. Call Victoria Plum 09882271

SUBURBAN DREAM. £45 ono. 0933322

SMELL THE COFFEE WITHOUT WAKING UP. Thlipperythlope.woosh

TIMELY MACHINE. Just like in books. Offers? Tel Moley.

BARELY PERCEPTIBLE DIFFERENCES. *£20 per dozen. Call D. J. Bowtie 0333 4365*

KILLER PUNCH. £7 per gallon. Send SAE to BOX 99

NON-SQUEAK PIPS. £11 per feline. Call Wiffle 0886423

END OF THE LINE. Would suit exasperated person. £160 ono. Tel. Gladys D'Arbanville 05578254

WAP ENABLED KITTENS. £80 per pair. To good, architecturally interesting home only. Call Diana Mania 0226.

CHARMLESS BRACELETS. Bespoke. £90–150. cha-cha@oompah.co.yk

GOLD STANDARD DOUBLE STANDARDS. Call for list. 014

CAREER-DEFINING ROLE, £250. Strong Supporting Cast, £150. £350 both. Tel. Alberta 04484678

WOMANISER. 70s model, still runs beautifully. £300 Tel. Mimi 0222984

ECCENTRICITY GAUGE. With Neo-Quirk LCD, doesn't work with uncles, hence £40. drcunningham@madprofessors.co.up

DONKADILLO. Unique hybrid. As stubborn and defensive as you are. £80. Tel Gwana 04485225

DIFFICULT DAYS. Traded. Call. I. Snow 0 0 0.

PANZERS. Good runners, tax exempt, still do the business. Tel. Jimbo 09976334

ORIGINAL COPIES. Used as new. POA, online application only—bream@oldnews.co-op

LIMITED EDITION SEAMUS HEANEY-STYLE

CLUB WEAR. Call for catalogue. Bog Duds 048453356

EXPECTATION GRATERS. Tireless Vehicles also. As used by Gary Newman and Gary Oldman. Call Fluid Exchange 08746225

ORIGINAL OLD CHESTNUT. Pristine condition. £17. Call Frank Phlegming 0922645

CRETIN AWARENESS COURSES. POD. Tel. Mel Influence. 011825554

FAIR TRADE PIXIES, available webly—panga@ethicalmythology.colon

VANILLA PRODS, £15. Call Huffers 05594245

MAKE SURE YOU OWN THE RIGHTS TO YOURSELF. Call for Hessian Bound Brochure. 033942323

SEASONAL BOTTOMS. £55 Call the Noel Coward of the County 04847444

FEAR. Needs servicing, still taxed. Bargain at £150. Tel. Vince.

PITHY INTERJECTIONS. £20 for eight. Tel Del 06695454

SOFTWARE VICTORIANA —teak, mahogany and elm digital interface. Quotes? 04483325

MICHAEL ATHERTON RINGTONES—*Still searching for that extra bit of swing, that was a real rip-snorter, I'm not sure how much of that the batsman saw and Matthew Hoggard!* Text WASTEMYLIFE to 079980

COLLECTABLES

ORIGINAL 1930S PROTESTANT WORK ETHIC, unwanted inheritance, hence £45 ono.

BERNARD INGHAM, needs attention. Only £25.

OGRES (breeder's cert included), family of four, would prefer to home together.

HIGHLY COLLECTABLE KIM IL SUNG 10" ACTION FIGURE (Mk III model includes eagle-eyes and realistic gripping hands), plus outfits—scuba diver, commando, indefatigable representative of the progressive proletariat. £80.

LIFE-SIZE JELLY HIPPOS (lemon & lime, mandarin, exotic fruits) £350 each.

FABERGÉ BUCKAROO, very rare, £8000 ovno.

FULL SERIES of Pablo Escobar's *Woodworker* magazine, with leatherette binder, £35.

CULTURE SHOCK ABSORBERS—re-conditioned, £40 per set.

CRETIN D'OR HANDBAG, genuine, £100.

DISTANT ARBOREAL SHADOWS. Never used. £5 each.

TERRORIST TOP TRUMPS —INLA, Baader-Meinhof, Shining Path, Al-Qaida. £5 each, £15 the set.

PUFF MUMMY, collector's item. POA.

FASHION WATER, mis en bouteille 2001. £10 per case.

WANTED

GALLOWS. Top prices paid. Call Donald. 01434 240500.

STUNT PUPPIES—minimum of 4 required. 0207 9118000.

MEDIEVAL SIEGE ARTILLERY. Will swap for orchard. 02830 263142.

NEW SYSTEM OF PHILOSOPHICAL THOUGHT. Will swap for Logical Positivism or Cartesian world view. Call Horst 0207 760 6500.

ILLEGAL DRUGS. Any type or quantity. Call Bez 0161 834 8730.

OXYGUM. Any price paid. Call Marine Boy 0207 306 0603.

VAGUE SENSE OF DIRECTION. singleman@hotmail.com

TUITION

TURTLE WAXING. Turtles supplied. £15 p.h. Call Leonardo 0207 428 4800.

BONGO SLACKENING (professional). £18 per day. Call Ali 0117 9741111.

CRASH YOUR CAR WITH STYLE. Call Jeremy 0208 752 6354.

JOBS

TREVOR EVE REPAIRS. Tibo 044633232

BAT RELEASING, shifts. £6.75 ph. 066751111

HER MAJESTY'S GOVERNMENT seeks a fellow, stout and true, to investigate the Bahamas. Contact speedgov.guv.ok

INTERNET DARNING, £12.50 ph, City & Guilds required. Call Alright Jobs 20202020

BRONTE marshal arts training, ha'penny per session. 0336721111

GIVE UP SMIRKING THE EASY WAY—glove therapy, driving, boxing, duelling. Tel Ian Ulean 000 435661

LOOK-ALIKES WANTED for highly original bank robbery/reality show: Ray Mears, Jeremy Clarkson, Andrew Marr, Cilla, Mick Hucknall. Tel 9990999

EARN UP TO £50 A DAY abusing free speech. Training given. Tel 6565656

THINK YOU CAN BRING LASTING PEACE TO THE MIDDLE EAST? £15 per hour. Call 0800 GODSWILL

SOMEONE REQUIRED TO WRITE 'EM LIKE THEY USED TO. Name your celery. Call Cole 0100200

WASP SITTER REQUIRED. 40 hours per week, salary negotiable, must have full UK driver's licence. Call 0208 743 8000.

FRIEND. Full-time. GSOH. ACA. LTR. BLT. PMT. CCCP. No time-wasters. Call 0161 200 2020.

GLASS ADMIRER. *Shifts —£10 per hour, applicant must have central nervous system. Call 0208 87525252.*

POPE. F/T with accommodation. Catholic preferred. Call 0207 588 3101.

SERVICES

LET SOMEONE ELSE FEEL THE GUILT. Box 022768888

CLUELESS PLUMBER—£3.50 ph. 0800BLEEP

EVER WONDERED WHO YOUR TRUE ENEMIES REALLY ARE? True Enemy Identification Provider. Call for consultation: 09996547

KNOBHEADS—£15 per dozen. 06755111

MEANDERING SERVICE, oddities provided. 044732323

TRY DONKEY WISDOM LTD—economic forecasting. Gnomic summarising also—double or quits. 055845555

STILL IN BED'S AN EXCELLENT ADVENTURE. 04757575

COLDPLAY REMOVAL. Experienced team available 24/8. 0998786

FEELING LIKE A LOLLARD? The medieval world is back. Moat diggers. 08897214

SUICIDE COACHING. All levels. 07575754

TOO BUSY TO ENJOY THE RELAXING SENSATION OF WATCHING YOUR TROPICAL FISH? Let us do it for you. PorcinatorX@jahoover.ja.

IF YOU THINK YOUR DOG IS LOOKING AT YOU IN AN IMPROPER FASHION, we can measure and certificate against government-recognised standards. 24-hour call-out. 047646411

DOES YOUR SENSE OF IRONY LET YOU DOWN? Have trouble quipping wryly? Find yourself meaning what you say rather too often? Get re-witted with *Dry Yourself Out*, the self-deprecating style-bible on DVD. 07000700

DOMESTIC VOID AVAILABLE. Unfurnished, deceptively spacious. £85 pw. 0448 4222

STILL GRINDING IT OUT? 03374765

Compiled by PAUL BARKER (Maidenhead), RICHARD TOMLIN (Hackney), DAVID HERD (Whitstable), IAN SANSOM (Bangor)

PERSONALS

RETIRED GENT, 68, into Tomb Raider and Doom, seeks Lara Croft look-alike with own bungalow. BOX784

MALE, LATE 40S, ex-forces, likes theatre, country pubs, visiting National Trust properties, seeks female, 30s, capable of calling in close air support on positions approximately 800 yards, repeat 800 yards, forward of the O.P. while pinned down by a withering small arms crossfire . . . if the need arises. BOX146

MELLOW GUY seeks Avril Lavigne type to rub me up the wrong way. BOX223

LADY, 42, likes theatre, cinema, poetry, ornate ceiling roses, seeks someone who's been to Uganda. BOX394

PALSIED OLD STEP-TAKER seeks foolish thin daydreamer to use it or not. BOX468

BADASS RAPPER, 24, seeks Jennie Murray type. Don't make me put a cap in yo ass! BOX372

MALE, 30s, made of gold, seeks mythological partner for country walks and nights in. BOX393

PSEUDO WRESTLER, 218, seeks breath of new fresh May in kiss with floating cherry blossom petal. BOX187

MY NAME REALLY IS BUCK ROGERS. Surely that's enough. BOX558

UGANDAN MAN, technically ancient, likes cinema, poetry and clean smooth modernist ceiling design, seeks similar. BOX395

ME AGAIN. BOX1

GASEOUS BLONDE, 25–40, seeks incendiary partner. BOX121

GENUINELY DANGEROUS GUY. Unstable behaviour and random acts of violence my speciality. Non-smoker. BOX432

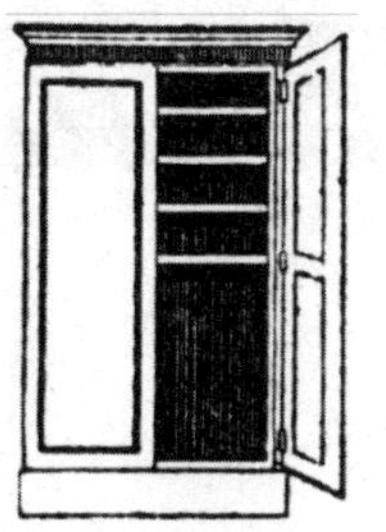

MAN, *40, GSOH, trapped in IKEA, Croydon. Please come and get me out. BOX679*

CHEF, 38, balsamic fundamentalist, seeks partner on a bed of genetically-enhanced super-cress, draped in a John Lewis-style duvet of hot and sour detritus. Make me drizzle liberally. BOX490

GOLD-DIGGER looking for gold mine, Baby! BOX997

LRB let you down?

theenthusiast@theenthusiast.co.uk

THE ENTHUSIAST, PO BOX 239, BANGOR, BT20 5YB

BEN COVE (*Manchester*)

A B C D E

F G H I J

K L M N O

S O R R Y

U V W X

Y Z

PICKARD TUSCAN DECORATED: *Pickard Jenkins*

– PRAYER CALENDAR –

I

Pray for GRIMSTON, CONGHAM, ROYDON.

II

Give thanks for the Department of Social Security.

III

Pray for the work of MAGAZINE EDITORS.

IV

Pray for AYLMERTON, RUNTON, EAST RUNTON, BEESTON REGIS, GRESHAM.

V

Pray for MELANESIA.

VI

Pray for ARNOLD SCHWARZENEGGER.

VII

Give thanks for the work of J.G. BALLARD.

VIII

Give thanks for the work of the Episcopal Church of CUBA.

IX

Pray for MALAITA (Solomon Isles): for the Melanesian Brothers held captive by the Guadalcanal Liberation Front.

X

For safety, for your FRIENDS.

XI

For MAMA IDRISSOU, cotton farmer, Tchaourou, BENIN.

XII

MALAYSIA. For Irene Fernandez, human rights activist.

XIII

For the FIVE BILLION living in slums.

XIV

LIBERIA. Pray for a political settlement, and for the relief work going on in the camps around Monrovia.

XV

ART. Pray for Damien Hirst.

XVI

NORTH KOREA. Pray for Kim Jong Il.

XVII

Pray for the work of teachers of PILATES.

XVIII

At this time of year, give thanks for FINGER BUFFETS.

XIX

Pray for FULL-TIME CARERS.

XX

Pray for PROFESSOR HERMIONE LEE, and her fellow judges of the 2006 Booker Prize for fiction.

XXI
Give thanks for BISHOP PETER LEE and
REVD. GILL LEE, from Potter Heigham,
working in SOUTH AFRICA.

XXII
Pray for PETER ACKROYD.

XXIII
Pray for ORGANISTS and BELLRINGERS.

XXIV
Give thanks for the EMERGENCY SERVICES.

XXV
For MUFFINS, give thanks.

XXVI
PAKISTAN. Remember and pray for the
family of journalist Amir Bakhsh Brohi,
murdered in Sindh province,
for reporting human rights violations.

XXVII
Remember also IRAN, for SHIRIN EBADI,
who won this year's Nobel Peace Prize.

XXVIII
For the makers of SOLAR PANELS.

XXIX
For wisdom, for WORLD LEADERS.

XXX
Thank God for TURKEY.

DONALD CONCORD *(Fife)*

What do you pray for?

theenthusiast@theenthusiast.co.uk THE ENTHUSIAST, PO BOX 239, BANGOR, BT20 5YB

– CORRECTIONS AND CLARIFICATIONS –

THERE are no more corrections and clarifications.

THE MOUSE OF THOUGHT—

Preparing layouts, reading proofs, sub-editing manuscripts and answering correspondence on the trestle-table set up in the shed, surrounded by the junk, the debris, the old bits of bike, and the vast damp messes of our own past excesses and pointless consumption, we glance upon a tin of Golden Virginia Ready Rubbed, worn smooth with use and full of rusty panel pins, and recall suddenly with a terrible pang the good advice offered to us by our parents and our parents' parents, which we seem too long to have neglected and forgotten: turn off your lights; and the kettle; save your vegetable water; buy nothing for your personal pleasure or comfort; use no transport and call on no labour unless urgent necessity compels; and before you travel always ask simply, 'Is my journey really necessary?'

The Enthusiast is a quarterly magazine.

To subscribe for 4 issues including postage:
UK: £25 — Ireland/Europe: €40 — USA: $50

Please make cheques payable to The Enthusiast. Or subscribe online at

www.theenthusiast.co.uk

Address for subscriptions and correspondence:
The Enthusiast, PO Box 239, Bangor, BT20 5YB.

Design and art direction: Valle Walkley

The Enthusiast is published in Bangor and Whitstable.